KITCHEN
TABLE

100 Pasta Recipes

The best recipes from your favourite chefs – now in your pocket!

- Download the app now and get 40 amazing recipes. Plus you can buy more recipes at any time – 340 more tasty dishes available in 7 carefully chosen collections.

- Clearly laid out recipes let you flick between introduction, ingredients and steps - plus you can create a shopping basket and share with friends at the touch of a button!

- Fully customisable search means you will always find a great recipe.

- You can also activate our revolutionary Touch-Free mode - perfect for when your hands are a little dirty in the kitchen.

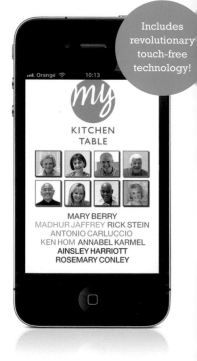

Includes revolutionary touch-free technology!

Find out more at www.mykitchentable.co.uk/app

KITCHEN TABLE

100 Pasta Recipes

ANTONIO CARLUCCIO

www.mykitchentable.co.uk

Welcome to **my** KITCHEN TABLE

This is my personal collection of the **100 tastiest** **most authentic Italian pasta dishes** you could wish for. Each one brings with it a little taste of the Mediterranean, and I hope you enjoy every bite

Contents

Fresh Egg Pasta

You can experiment using different flours here, but I think Italian 00 flour (*farina* 00 or *doppio zero*) is the easiest to work with by hand.

Step one Sift the flour onto a work surface (marble is ideal), forming it into a volcano-shaped mound with a well in the centre. Break the eggs into the well and add the salt. Incorporate the eggs into the flour with your hands, gradually drawing the flour into the egg mixture until it forms a coarse paste. Add a little more flour if the mixture is too soft or sticky and, with a spatula, scrape up any pieces of dough. Before kneading the dough, clean your hands and the work surface.

Step two Lightly flour the work surface, and start to knead with the heel of one hand. Work the dough for 10–15 minutes until the consistency is smooth and elastic. Wrap the dough in clingfilm or foil and allow it to rest for half an hour.

Step three Again, lightly flour your work surface and a rolling pin. Gently roll out the dough, rotating it in quarter turns to a sheet 3mm (less than ¼in) in thickness. If you are making filled pasta, go straight ahead and incorporate the filling as in the recipes. If you are making flat pasta or shapes, leave the pasta on a clean tea towel to dry for about half an hour before cutting.

If you wish, you can also add one of the colourings suggested in the ingredients list, though you may need to increase the proportion of flour to eggs slightly so that your mixture doesn't become too wet. If you choose to make pasta purpurea, use only 2 eggs.

Makes about 450g (1lb)

300g (11oz) Italian 00 flour, plus extra for dusting

3 medium eggs

pinch of salt

for pasta *verde* (green pasta)

75g (3oz) well-drained puréed cooked spinach

for pasta *purpurea* (purple pasta)

4 tbsp beetroot juice

for pasta *rossa* (red pasta)

1½ tbsp tomato purée

for pasta *neri* (black pasta)

1 tsp cuttlefish ink

For a video masterclass on making fresh pasta, go to www.mykitchentable.co.uk/videos/makingpasta

Minestrone

There are many different varieties of minestrone, each one varying according to regional customs. I'll allow you to substitute a stock cube for home-made stock in this recipe, but only if you really have to!

Serves 4

3 tbsp olive oil

1 onion, peeled and chopped

1 small garlic clove, peeled and chopped

2 rashers streaky bacon, rinded and finely chopped, or 25g (1oz) Parma ham, finely chopped (optional)

4 celery sticks, diced

1 tomato, peeled, de-seeded and finely chopped

1 large carrot, peeled and diced

2 potatoes, peeled and diced

few leaves basil, or 1 tbsp pesto sauce

900ml (1½ pints) chicken stock

1 x 375g (13oz) tin borlotti beans, drained

100g (4oz) *tubettini* (fresh or dried)

75g (3oz) freshly grated Parmesan

salt and freshly ground black pepper

Step one Heat the oil and fry the onion and garlic with the chopped bacon or Parma ham (if using), until the onion is soft. Add the remaining vegetables, the basil or pesto, and toss well with the oil. Add the stock and bring to the boil. Cook for around 10 minutes. Add salt and pepper to taste and stir in the borlotti beans and the pasta. Cook for about 10 minutes, or until the pasta is al dente. Serve hot, sprinkled with the grated Parmesan.

Spaghettini with Tomato and Basil

This is one of the simplest sauces. If you use garlic instead of onion, and olive oil instead of butter, you obtain a Neapolitan sauce that is equally good. If you manage to find the best ripe tomatoes, you can leave out the cheese because the taste will be rich and fine without it.

Step one Heat the butter and gently fry the onion or spring onions until beginning to brown. Add the tomatoes and fry for another 3–4 minutes. Add the basil and salt to taste.

Step two Meanwhile, cook the pasta according to the packet instructions or until al dente. Mix with the sauce and serve sprinkled with the grated Parmesan.

Serves 4

50g (2oz) butter

1 small onion, peeled and finely chopped, or 4 spring onions, trimmed and finely chopped

3 large, ripe tomatoes, peeled, de-seeded and roughly chopped

8 basil leaves, shredded

400g (14oz) spaghettini (fresh or dried)

50g (2oz) freshly grated Parmesan

salt

Spaghettini with Seafood Sauce

Almost everywhere, and especially in seaside restaurants in Italy, you can find this dish, which is made with any kind of local, fresh, small mollusc or fish. You can use a small octopus, squid, mussels, clams, oysters, small prawns or scallops. If you are using clams or mussels, make sure you clean them thoroughly. In some areas of Italy they add tomatoes, but I prefer it without.

Serves 4

6 tbsp olive oil

1 garlic clove, peeled and finely chopped

1 chilli pepper, finely chopped (optional)

350g (12oz) mixed seafood (as suggested above), cleaned

2 tbsp dry white wine

375g (13oz) spaghettini (fresh or dried)

1 tbsp finely chopped flat-leaf parsley

salt and freshly ground black pepper

Step one Heat the oil and gently fry the garlic, and chilli, if using, until the garlic is slightly golden. Add the seafood, increase the heat and fry for 8–10 minutes, stirring continuously. Make sure that the clams and mussels are open at the end of the cooking time. If they are not, discard them. Pour in the wine and let it evaporate for 1 minute. Keep the mixture warm over a low heat and add salt and pepper to taste.

Step two Meanwhile, cook the fresh or dried pasta according to the packet instructions or until al dente, and drain. Mix with the sauce. Serve sprinkled with the parsley.

Spaghetti Carbonara

I include a recipe for this well-known dish because most people I know get it completely wrong, either adding milk or cream or letting the eggs become scrambled. This recipe is the real thing. It was brought to Lazio from Umbria by coal men (*carbonari*), who came to sell charcoal to the Romans. Since then it has been adopted by the Romans and is famous all over the world.

Step one Cook the pasta in a large pan of boiling salted water according to the packet instructions or until al dente. Meanwhile, heat the lard, butter and oil in a pan and fry the garlic and pancetta or *guanciale* until crisp. Discard the garlic and add the white wine to the pan. Boil to evaporate it a little.

Step two Lightly beat the eggs in a large bowl with the grated Parmesan, parsley and some salt and pepper. When the pasta is ready, drain and add to the egg mixture in the bowl, stirring to coat the pasta. Then add to the pancetta or *guanciale* in the pan. Stir a couple of times and then serve.

Caution *This recipe contains lightly cooked eggs.*

Serves 6

500g (1lb 2oz) spaghetti or spaghettoni (the largest spaghetti) (fresh or dried)

25g(1oz) lard

25g (1oz) butter

2 tbsp olive oil

1 garlic clove, slightly squashed

100g (4oz) pancetta or *guanciale*, cut into small chunks

5 tbsp dry white wine

5 eggs

100g (4oz) freshly grated Parmesan (or pecorino cheese for the purists)

3 tbsp finely chopped parsley

salt and freshly ground black pepper

Linguine with Tuna Fish Sauce

The flat, slightly rounded shape of this pasta particularly suits sauces based on fish. This recipe just goes to show how useful it is to keep a tin of tuna in the cupboard.

Serves 4

4 tbsp virgin olive oil

3 tbsp finely chopped parsley

2 garlic cloves, peeled and finely chopped

1 small chilli pepper, finely chopped

1cm (½ in) fresh root ginger, peeled and thinly sliced

450g (1lb) passata or chopped tomatoes

1 x 400g (14oz) tin tuna fish in oil, drained and roughly chopped

375g (13oz) linguine (fresh or dried)

salt and freshly ground black pepper

Step one Heat the oil and gently fry 2 tablespoons of the parsley, the garlic, chilli and the ginger for a few minutes until slightly soft. Add the tomatoes and continue to cook for another few minutes. Stir in the tuna and a little salt.

Step two Meanwhile, cook the fresh or dried pasta according to the packet instructions or until al dente, and drain. Toss with the sauce and serve sprinkled with the remaining parsley and freshly ground pepper to taste.

Ravioli with Spinach and Ricotta

The ravioli in this recipe are square (you can make round ravioli too, called *tortelli*), and different sizes are called raviolini, ravioli and ravioloni respectively, from the smallest to the largest. This simple dish is delicious with a fresh tomato sauce.

Step one Cook the spinach in a little water, then drain well. Squeeze out the excess moisture and roughly chop, then mix with the ricotta cheese. Stir in the nutmeg, seasoning, egg yolks and 25g (1oz) of the Parmesan.

Step two Roll out the pasta dough on a lightly floured surface to give two pasta sheets about 3mm (less than ¼in) thick and both about 37 x 23cm (14½ x 9in) in size. Put heaped teaspoons of the filling on one sheet of pasta, 5cm (2in) apart. Cover with the other sheet of pasta. Press gently with your fingers all round the filling to seal the ravioli shapes, without air bubbles. Cut the pasta into squares with a pastry wheel, and lay the ravioli on a tea towel.

Step three Cook the pasta in boiling salted water for around 4–5 minutes or until al dente. Meanwhile, melt the butter. Drain the pasta and mix it with the butter. Scatter with sage and serve with the remaining Parmesan.

Serves 4

250g (9oz) fresh spinach

140g (5oz) ricotta cheese

2 tsp freshly grated nutmeg

2 egg yolks

85g (3oz) freshly grated Parmesan

450g (1lb) fresh pasta dough (see page 7)

85g (3oz) unsalted butter

4 sage leaves, finely chopped

salt and freshly ground black pepper

For a video masterclass on filling pasta, go to
www.mykitchentable.co.uk/videos/fillingpasta

Taglierini with Three Mushrooms

Fresh chanterelles and morels are in season during the spring and early summer and are now available in most large supermarkets. Fresh ceps are available from August until late October. If you can't find the fresh variety, I suggest you use 25g (1oz) each of any two of the mushrooms in their dried form and add 100g (4oz) cultivated oyster mushrooms. If you do this, you will need to soak the dried mushrooms in warm water for around 20 minutes before using.

Serves 4

85g (3oz) butter

1 small onion, finely chopped

55g (2oz) Parma ham, finely chopped

115g (4oz) fresh chanterelles, sliced

115g (4oz) fresh morels, sliced

115g (4oz) fresh ceps, sliced

300g (10½ oz) fresh taglierini

85g (3oz) freshly grated Parmesan

salt and freshly ground black pepper

Step one Heat the butter and fry the onion until golden. Add the Parma ham, fry for a few minutes, then add the mushrooms and a little salt and cook for a few minutes until the mushrooms are just softening.

Step two Cook the pasta in boiling salted water for 20 seconds then drain, reserving 1–2 tablespoons of the cooking water. Toss the pasta with the mushrooms and a little of the cooking water just to moisten and add salt and pepper to taste. Sprinkle with Parmesan to serve.

Trofie with Pesto

Trofie is a particular pasta shape from Liguria. It is usually home-made but you can find it in good Italian shops. Alternatively, you can use *strozzapreti* or fusilli instead.

Step one Put the garlic and basil leaves in a mortar and add the salt, which under the pestle and the power of your elbow will function as a grinder. Also add the pine kernels and reduce to a paste, slowly drizzling in some oil. Incorporate the Parmesan and continue to grind with the pestle, adding enough oil to achieve a very smooth and homogenous sauce of a brilliant green colour.

Step two Boil the pasta in slightly salted water according to the packet instructions. Drain, transfer to a pre-warmed china bowl and mix thoroughly with the pesto sauce. Serve immediately. The sauce should cover each piece of pasta and there should be none left on the plate!

Serves 4

4 garlic cloves

40–50 basil leaves

10g (¼ oz) coarse sea salt

50g (2oz) pine kernels

extra-virgin olive oil, as required

50g (2oz) freshly grated Parmesan

500g (1¼ lb) dried trofie, *strozzapreti* or fusilli

For a video masterclass on using a pestle and mortar, go to
www.mykitchentable.co.uk/videos/pestlemortar

Penne Rigate with Sausage

The ribbed penne rigate are very popular in Italy, and abroad too. Usually, an Italian trattoria offers them *all'arrabbiata* – with chilli or with a tuna-fish sauce. (They are also used in timbales.) This version is based on the best-quality pork sausage meat you can find (100 per cent pork, if possible) and it is very delicious.

Serves 4

75g (3oz) butter

1 small onion, peeled and chopped

1 garlic clove, peeled and finely chopped

300g (11oz) pork sausage meat or sausages (*luganega* type)

1 sprig rosemary, finely chopped

150ml (5fl oz) dry white wine

pinch of freshly grated nutmeg

pinch of ground cloves

375g (13oz) dried penne rigate or penne

75g (3oz) freshly grated Parmesan

salt and freshly ground black pepper

Step one Heat the butter and gently fry the onion and the garlic. Break up the sausage meat with a fork (if using sausages, remove the skin before breaking up the meat). Add to the pan and gently fry until well browned. Add the rosemary and the wine, and cook slowly for 10 minutes. Add the nutmeg, cloves and a little salt and pepper.

Step two Cook the pasta for 7–8 minutes or until al dente, and drain. Mix with the sausage mixture and the Parmesan.

Cannelloni

It is well known all over the world that cannelloni can be made in thousands of ways. Fillings are made from meat, fish or vegetables or a mixture. In principle, the filling is wrapped in a small sheet of cooked pasta, then baked with a tomato sauce.

Step one Preheat the oven to 220°C/425°F/gas 7. If using dried ceps, soak in warm water for 20 minutes, drain and reserve the soaking liquid. Squeeze dry and finely chop.

Step two Make the cannelloni. Roll out the pasta dough on a lightly floured surface to make two sheets of pasta, each 25cm (10in) square and 3mm (less than ¼in) thick. Cut each sheet into four squares and lay on a clean tea towel. Cook the pasta for 4 minutes, adding the squares one by one to plenty of boiling water containing the tablespoon of oil to prevent them sticking. Carefully remove the pasta, using a slotted spoon, and pat dry on a clean tea towel.

Step three Make the filling. Heat the butter and fry the onion until soft. Add the beef and ceps and fry until the beef is browned. Add salt, pepper and nutmeg to taste and set aside to cool slightly. Stir the egg yolk and parsley into the filling mixture and mix together well. Divide the filling between the pasta squares, spooning it down the middle of each piece. Place a mozzarella segment on top of the filling and roll the pasta squares round the filling to make cannelloni tubes. Place 2 tablespoons of the tomato sauce in the base of a large ovenproof dish. Lay the cannelloni, side by side, over the sauce and cover with the remaining sauce. Sprinkle with the Parmesan and bake for around 20 minutes until golden.

You can use dried cannelloni which are ready to be filled but, if you do, allow extra cooking time (see packet for instructions). Many people like to use a white sauce with cheese added to cover the cannelloni before baking, but I find this a little rich so I have not included it here. But if you like, top with a sauce.

Serves 4

25g (1oz) dried ceps or 200g (7oz) fresh ceps, finely chopped

450g (1lb) fresh pasta dough (see page 7 or see the tip below)

1 tbsp olive oil

50g (2oz) butter

1 onion, very finely sliced

400g (14oz) lean minced beef

pinch of freshly grated nutmeg

1 egg yolk

2 tbsp finely chopped parsley

1 mozzarella cheese, drained and cut into 8 segments

1 quantity tomato sauce (see page 35)

75g (3oz) freshly grated Parmesan

salt and freshly ground black pepper

Tortellini with Cream

Tortellini are nothing else than a smaller version of tortelloni. Old women in the region of Emilia Romagna, towards the north of Italy, make tortellini which are very small indeed. I have never discovered how they can turn the tortellini, or *cappelletti*, as they are known there, around their fingers.

Serves 6

100g (4oz) lean pork

100g (4oz) chicken or turkey breast

100g (4oz) beef marrow, extracted from the bone (optional)

75g (3oz) butter

75g (3oz) Parma ham

100g (4oz) mortadella

3 tbsp chopped parsley

225g (8oz) freshly grated Parmesan

¾ tsp freshly grated nutmeg

3 eggs, lightly beaten

675g (1½ lb) fresh pasta dough (see page 7)

150ml (5fl oz) double cream

salt and freshly ground black pepper

Step one Roughly chop the pork, chicken or turkey, and the marrow (if using). Heat the butter and fry the meats until brown. Put the meats in a food-processor with the Parma ham, mortadella and parsley and blend to a smooth paste. Fold 150g (5oz) of the Parmesan into the paste. Stir in the nutmeg, eggs, salt and plenty of black pepper. Mix well, cover and leave the filling to stand for 1–2 hours.

Step two To make the tortelloni, roll out the pasta dough on a lightly floured surface to 3mm (less than ¼in) thickness. Using a knife, cut out squares 5cm (2in) in size. Place a teaspoonful of filling in the centre of each square, fold one corner over to make a triangle, and press the edges lightly together. Gently bring the corners of the triangles together to make circular shapes. Lay the tortelloni on a clean tea towel.

Step three Cook the pasta for 5–6 minutes and drain. Toss well in the double cream, and gently heat through. Serve simply with plenty of black pepper.

Vegetarian Lasagne

This is a wonderful dish which will fully justify the effort involved.

Step one Preheat the oven to 190°C/375°F/gas 5. To make the lasagne, roll out the pasta dough (if using fresh) on a lightly floured surface to make a single sheet 3mm (less than ¼in) thick. Cut into rectangles about 10 x 20cm (4 x 8in) in size. Cook the fresh or dried pasta, adding the pieces one by one to boiling water to which you have added salt and 1 tablespoon oil. Allow 5 minutes cooking time for fresh pasta, 8–10 minutes for dried. Carefully remove the pasta and pat dry on clean tea towels.

Step two To make the spinach balls, cook the spinach in water until tender, drain and chop. Mix the spinach with 1 tablespoon beaten egg, the breadcrumbs and 25g (1oz) of the Parmesan. Add nutmeg, salt and pepper to taste. Using your hands, shape the spinach mixture into walnut-sized balls. Heat enough oil to deep-fry the spinach balls, until lightly browned on all sides.

Step three To prepare the aubergines, slice them lengthways into 5mm (¼in) slices, then put half of the 2 beaten eggs in a dish. Dip the aubergine into the flour, then the eggs. Heat enough oil to deep-fry the aubergine, until golden. Remove the aubergines from the heat and prepare the courgettes in the same way, dipping them into flour and beaten egg, then deep-frying.

Step four To prepare the mushrooms, heat 1 tablespoon oil in a frying pan, add the mushroom slices and fry briefly. Chop and stir in the garlic and parsley, with salt and pepper to taste.

Step five To assemble, put 3–4 tablespoons of tomato sauce in a baking dish. Cover with a layer of pasta, then add a layer each of the mushrooms, courgettes, aubergine and spinach balls. Add some chunks of the fontina or Taleggio cheese. Now add 3–4 tablespoons tomato sauce, 3–4 tablespoons of the 7 beaten eggs, and a sprinkle of the remaining Parmesan. Starting with another layer of pasta, repeat the layers until the ingredients are all used, finishing with a layer of vegetables and cheeses. Bake in the preheated oven for 20 minutes and serve.

Serves 6–8

550g (1¼lb) fresh pasta verde dough (see page 7) or 1lb (450g) dried green lasagne

olive oil

1.5kg (3lb) spinach

1 egg, lightly beaten (for the spinach)

2 tbsp breadcrumbs

150g (5oz) freshly grated Parmesan

freshly grated nutmeg

2 large aubergines

2 eggs, lightly beaten (for coating the vegetables)

100g (4oz) white flour

2 large courgettes

300g (11oz) fresh oyster mushrooms or shiitake mushrooms, sliced

1 garlic clove

1 tbsp parsley

double quantity tomato sauce (see page 35)

300g (11oz) fontina or Taleggio cheese

7 eggs, lightly beaten (for assembling the lasagne)

salt and freshly ground pepper

Baked Pasta

This is a dish for grand occasions, such as weddings or Christmas. Some gourmet Neapolitans add fresh truffles, but personally I think that is going a little too far . . .

Serves 8

800g (1¾lb) pasta, such as maccheroni, *ziti* or penne (fresh or dried)

450g (1lb) mozzarella cheese, cut into small cubes

200g (7oz) freshly grated Parmesan

for the sauce

400g (14oz) fresh porcini, chopped or 400g (14oz) of cultivated mushrooms plus 25g (1oz) dried porcini

100ml (3½ fl oz) olive oil

1 onion, finely chopped

1 garlic clove, finely chopped

500g (1lb 2oz) chicken livers and hearts

1 small glass white wine

1kg (2¼ lb) ripe tomatoes, de-seeded and chopped

handful of chopped basil

salt and freshly ground black pepper

Step one For the sauce, soak the dried porcini mushrooms in warm water for 30 minutes, then drain them. Heat the oil in a large pan and fry the onion and garlic until softened. Add the chicken livers and hearts and cook over a medium heat for 15 minutes, stirring all the time. Add the mushrooms and cook for a few minutes. Pour in the wine and boil to evaporate a little. Add the tomatoes and basil and cook gently for 40 minutes. Season to taste.

Step two Preheat the oven to 200°C/400°F/gas 6. Cook the pasta in a large pan of boiling salted water for half its normal cooking time, then drain and mix with a little of the sauce. Take a round or square 25–30cm (10–12in) baking tin or ovenproof dish about 7.5cm (3in) deep and, commencing with pasta, build layers of pasta and sauce, scattering mozzarella cubes and grated Parmesan in between. Finish with sauce and Parmesan. Bake for 25 minutes and then serve.

Tomato Sauce

There are many ways to make a tomato sauce. This is a very basic and quick version, but it makes an excellent standby when hunger beats the clock!

Step one Heat the butter or oil in a pan and fry the onion until soft. Add the tomatoes and cook gently for 10 minutes. Stir in the basil, season with salt and pepper and cook for another 5 minutes.

Variation

1 celery stick, finely chopped

1 tbsp chopped parsley

1 garlic clove, peeled and finely chopped

Add the above ingredients when frying the onion and continue as before.

Serves 4

25g (1oz) butter or 2 tbsp olive oil

1 large onion, peeled and finely chopped

1 x 400g (14oz) tin chopped tomatoes

6 basil leaves, chopped

salt and freshly ground black pepper

Bolognese Sauce

One of the best-known Italian recipes abroad, Spaghetti Bolognese does not exist in Italy. It is something you will find in a restaurant run by non-Italians or by Italians not in touch with genuine Italian food. The real thing is called Tagliatelle *al Ragù* and comes from Bologna in Emilia Romagna. Genuine *Ragù Bolognese* is a combination of at least two types of meat, like lean minced beef and pork, plus oil and butter, a little wine, an onion, plump ripe tomatoes and tomato paste. The sprinkling of freshly grated Parmesan perfectly crowns this very Emilian dish.

Serves 4

25g (1oz) butter

2 tbsp olive oil

1 medium-sized onion, chopped

250g (9oz) minced beef

250g (9oz) minced pork

6 tbsp white wine

1 tsp concentrated tomato purée

1kg (2¼ lb) passata or chopped tomatoes

salt and freshly ground black pepper

Step one Heat the butter and oil in a pan and fry the chopped onion. Then add the meat and fry until golden brown. Stir in the wine, tomato purée and passata or chopped tomatoes. Season with salt and pepper to taste. Cover with a lid and leave to simmer for about 2 hours, stirring from time to time. Serve with freshly cooked tagliatelle and sprinkle with freshly grated Parmesan, if desired, but purists like this dish without.

Have you made this recipe? Tell us what you think at
www.mykitchentable.co.uk/blog

Mushroom Sauce

There are many versions of this sauce. I have written about some of them in my earlier books, but over the years my taste has evolved. Because the wild season is short, you may be obliged to use cultivated mushrooms, although these do not give the same depth of taste. Remember, you should always consult a reliable reference book before picking wild mushrooms. Below are two versions of sauces with mushrooms, one white and one red.

Step one Soak the dried mushrooms in the tepid water for 30 minutes and squeeze dry, reserving the soaking liquor. Heat the oil and fry the rosemary and garlic for 20 seconds. If you are making the red sauce, add the extra oil at this point. Add the fresh mushrooms and soaked dried mushrooms and continue to cook for 15 minutes, stirring from time to time.

Step two For the white sauce, stir in the soaking liquor and the butter and cook for a further 15 minutes. Serve with pasta, rice or on meat *scaloppine.* For the red sauce, stir in the passata or chopped tomatoes and the tomato purée and cook over a moderate heat for a further 15-20 minutes. Serve with polenta.

Serves 4

25g (1oz) dried porcini mushrooms or mixed with dried morels

150ml (5fl oz) tepid water

8 tbsp extra-virgin olive oil

1 sprig rosemary

1 garlic clove, finely chopped

400g (14oz) fresh mushrooms (e.g. field, hedgehog and oyster), cut into bite-sized pieces

salt and freshly ground black pepper

for the white sauce

15g (½ oz) butter

for the red sauce

2–3 tbsp extra-virgin olive oil

4 tbsp passata or chopped tomatoes

1 tbsp tomato purée

Herb Sauce

This is my recipe for herb sauce. Please try it and vary it according to your taste, increasing one or other of the herbs, or taking away one altogether. The important thing is that you cook it to your taste. Like pesto, it can be used for a variety of savoury pasta dishes.

Serves 4

½ small onion, finely chopped

4 tbsp extra-virgin olive oil

100g (4oz) butter

1 garlic clove, finely chopped

25g (1oz) pine kernels

8 tbsp very finely chopped mixed herbs (chervil, parsley, chives, basil, mint, sage, rosemary and fennel leaves)

2 tbsp chicken or vegetable stock

grated zest ½ lime

salt and freshly ground black pepper

Step one Fry the onion gently in the oil and half the butter until soft without colouring. Add the garlic and pine kernels and fry for 2 minutes. Stir in the herbs, stock, lime zest, the remaining butter and season to taste and serve. Be quick as it is vital you do not 'cook' the herbs but just warm them up.

Tomato and Meat Ragout

Another indispensable recipe. Although it takes some time to cook this sauce, the actual preparation is very easy and it is very tasty. The best result is achieved by using a piece of pork and a piece of lamb, both on the bone, but any combination, or all of one meat, will do. The result is a deliciously condensed sauce which we would eat with our pasta, to be followed by the meat as a main course. If you want the meat to serve 4 as a main course, increase it to 1kg (2¼lb) all told.

Step one Heat the butter or oil in a heavy-based pan and fry the onion until soft. Add the meat and fry for several minutes until browned. Add the wine and continue cooking for 2–3 minutes. Stir in the tomatoes, cover and simmer very gently for 1½ hours. Stir the contents from time to time. If the sauce becomes too dry add a little water. When the sauce has been simmered for around 1½ hours, add the basil, salt and pepper, and cook uncovered for another 30 minutes.

Serves 4

25g (1oz) butter or
2 tbsp olive oil

1 large onion, peeled
and finely chopped

275g (10oz) lamb, beef
or pork with bone

150ml (5fl oz) red wine

2 x 400g (14oz) tins
chopped tomatoes

6 basil leaves,
chopped

salt and freshly ground
black pepper

Sardinian Risotto

This risotto does not differ much in principle from the Spanish paella. Considering that Sardinia and Catalonia have many things in common, including some dialect, this is not so surprising. It is, however, very different from the northern Italian risotto.

Serves 6

6 tbsp olive oil

600g (1lb 5oz) risotto rice

75g (3oz) aged pecorino cheese, grated

40g (1½oz) butter

freshly ground black pepper

for the ragù

4 tbsp olive oil

1 small onion, finely chopped

250g (9oz) minced lean pork or veal

1 small glass red wine (preferably Sardinian Cannonau)

200ml (7fl oz) chicken stock

200g (7oz) passata or chopped tomatoes

¼ tsp good saffron powder

salt

Step one First make the *ragù*. Heat the oil in a pan, add the onion and fry gently until softened. Then add the minced meat and fry until brown. Stir in the wine, stock, passata or chopped tomatoes, saffron and some salt and simmer for 20–25 minutes. Remove from the heat and set the *ragù* aside.

Step two For the risotto, heat the oil in a pan, add the rice and stir for about 5 minutes over a gentle heat to coat each grain with oil. Gradually add half the *ragù* and stir for 5 minutes. Keep an eye on the moisture level and add some hot water if necessary; the rice will absorb a lot of liquid. Add the rest of the *ragù* and stir for around 10 minutes or until the rice is cooked. The consistency should be quite loose. Stir in the grated cheese, butter and some pepper. Leave to rest for a few minutes and then serve.

Soup with Pasta

This is the simplest of all soups – it is very much used in northern Italy, especially for the evening meal, when it is warming, but not too heavy. It is based on very good, home-made chicken stock. Do not use stock cubes to hurry the process.

Step one Bring the stock to the boil, add the tomato and cook for a few minutes. Add the pasta and cook for another 3–5 minutes. Taste and add salt if necessary. Serve hot sprinkled with the Parmesan and chives.

Serves 4

1.2 litres (2 pints) chicken stock

1 ripe tomato, peeled, de-seeded and finely chopped

150g (5oz) dried *capelli d'angelo* or spaghetti

25g (1oz) freshly grated Parmesan

2 tsp finely chopped chives

salt

Soup with Cappelletti

You'll find it easier to use dried pasta for this recipe, rather than making your own. However, if you do decide to make your own (see page 7) or you manage to find some fresh *cappelletti* or *raviolini*, use 250g (9oz) and cook it for 5–7 minutes.

Serves 4

1.2 litres (2 pints) chicken stock

1 ripe tomato, peeled, de-seeded and finely chopped

150g (5oz) dried *cappelletti* or *raviolini*

25g (1oz) freshly grated Parmesan

2 tsp coarsely chopped celery or a few leaves flat-leaf parsley

Step one Bring the stock to the boil, add the tomato and cook for a few minutes. Add the pasta and cook for another 7–12 minutes. Serve hot, sprinkled with the Parmesan and either the celery or the parsley.

Peasant Soup

This is my own version of a peasant soup which is also enjoyed in some of the best restaurants all over Italy. For this dish, the Neapolitans use pasta called *munnezzaglia* which is all the leftovers from different packets of pasta – for a quick meal, you can simply break spaghetti into smaller pieces. To speed up the preparation of this dish I suggest using tinned beans instead of dried.

Step one Heat the oil and sweat the garlic. Add the vegetables and toss well. Pour in the stock, bring to the boil and simmer for 5 minutes. Add half the beans. Mash the remaining beans to a pulp with the back of a fork and add to the stock with the pasta, the chilli and the basil. Cook gently for another 8 minutes, stirring from time to time to prevent the mixture sticking. Serve with a trickle of oil on top.

Serves 4

2 tbsp olive oil

2 garlic cloves, peeled and finely chopped

1 carrot, peeled and diced

2 potatoes, peeled and diced

1 celery stick, diced

1 large tomato, peeled, de-seeded and diced

1.2 litres (2 pints) chicken stock

2 x 375g (13oz) tins cannellini or borlotti beans, drained

200g (7oz) *munnezzaglia* or spaghetti, broken into pieces

1 small chilli pepper, finely chopped

2 basil leaves, shredded

1 tbsp virgin olive oil

salt and freshly ground black pepper

Pasta Salad with Vegetables

This is a very tasty summertime dish that brings out the delicate flavour of the vegetables.

Serves 4

200g (7oz) asparagus, trimmed

200g (7oz) celeriac, cut into large matchsticks

300g (11oz) dried *gomiti*, *sedanoni* or penne

6 tbsp virgin olive oil

2 tbsp white wine vinegar

2 very large tomatoes, skinned, de-seeded and roughly chopped

200g (7oz) mozzarella cheese, diced

100g (4oz) pecorino cheese, cut into strips

2 tbsp finely chopped basil

salt and freshly ground black pepper

Step one Cook the asparagus and the celeriac separately in slightly salted, boiling water until tender, allowing about 20 minutes. Drain and leave to cool. Cut the asparagus into 2.5cm (1in) pieces.

Step two Cook the pasta in boiling salted water for 7 minutes or until slightly softer than al dente. Drain and leave to cool slightly.

Step three In a bowl, mix together the oil and vinegar, and season with salt and pepper. Stir in the tomatoes, mozzarella and pecorino cheeses, celeriac, asparagus and basil. Mix well, add the pasta and stir to combine. Check seasoning and serve cold or slightly warm.

Pasta Salad with Fish

The best anchovies are whole anchovies preserved in salt from delicatessens. They give the best flavour, but if you can't get these use tinned, filleted anchovies in oil. Drain before using.

Step one If using salted anchovies, soak in water for 30 minutes. Dry on kitchen paper and remove any large bones, then cut the fillets into pieces.

Step two Cook the pasta in boiling salted water for 7 minutes or until slightly softer than al dente, then drain well and leave to cool. Cook the squid in boiling salted water for 5 minutes, drain and leave to cool.

Step three In a bowl, mix together the oil, lemon juice, salt and pepper. Add the cooked squid, anchovies, smoked salmon, prawns, chives and dill and mix well. Add the pasta, stir well and taste again for seasoning. Serve cold.

Serves 4

10 anchovy fillets, salted or in oil (see introduction)

300g (11oz) dried farfalle or conchiglie

200g (7oz) squid, cleaned and cut into strips

6 tbsp virgin olive oil

juice of 1 lemon

100g (4oz) smoked salmon, cut into strips

200g (7oz) small cooked and peeled prawns, thawed if frozen

3 tbsp finely snipped chives

3 tbsp finely chopped dill

salt and freshly ground black pepper

Pasta with Peas

This dish was made by my mother as soon as the very tender and sweet, new season peas were available; it can also be made with very fresh broad beans. She used to make a plain pasta, from just flour and water, purposely for this dish so that when cooked it had a marvellously soft texture. I suggest you use a large and possibly flat type of eggless pasta and cook it a little longer than usual, so that you achieve the same softness. Don't use tinned peas for this recipe; if you can't find fresh peas then use frozen ones.

Serves 4

3 tbsp olive oil

1 small onion, peeled and finely sliced

50g (2oz) cooked ham, cut into very thin strips

300g (11oz) podded fresh garden peas (or broad beans)

1.2 litres (2 pints) chicken stock

200g (7oz) dried lasagne or pappardelle, broken into pieces

6 basil leaves, chopped

salt and freshly ground black pepper

Step one Heat the oil and fry the onion until soft, then add the ham, the peas and the stock and cook for 10 minutes or until the peas are soft. Add the pasta and the basil, taste and add salt and pepper, and cook for another 10 minutes until the pasta is soft.

For more recipes from My Kitchen Table, sign up for our newsletter at www.mykitchentable.co.uk/newsletter

Pasta Omelette

There is no *Pasquetta* (Easter Monday) for many Italian families without a *frittata di maccheroni*. On this day, weather permitting, everybody takes this dish with them on a picnic, wherever they are – in the country, at the beach, or in the mountains. For me it brings back pleasurable childhood memories of days out of doors with my family.

Step one Heat half the oil in a large, deep frying pan, add the pasta and heat thoroughly. Stir the Parmesan, parsley, salt and pepper, and the beaten eggs into the pasta and fry gently until a crust forms on the bottom of the pasta. Invert the pasta omelette onto a plate and then put back in the pan, adding the remainder of the oil to cook the other side. Serve hot or cold.

Serves 4–6

6 tbsp olive oil

1 quantity cooked spaghettini or linguine

50g (2oz) freshly grated Parmesan

4 tbsp finely chopped flat-leaf parsley

6 eggs, lightly beaten

salt and freshly ground black pepper

Angel's Hair with Lemon

An extremely delicate fresh pasta deserves a delicate sauce. *Capelli d'angelo*, or angel's hair, is practically the finest cut of pasta you can obtain either by machine or by hand. It cooks in less than a minute, so when you put the pasta on the hob make sure everyone is ready to eat! If you can't find *capelli d'angelo*, use a thin spaghetti instead.

Serves 4

50g (2oz) unsalted butter

3 tbsp double cream, with a little milk if necessary

finely grated zest and juice of ½ lemon

450g (1lb) *capelli d'angelo* or spaghetti (fresh or dried)

50g (2oz) freshly grated Parmesan

sprigs of parsley, to garnish (optional)

salt and freshly ground black pepper

Step one Gently melt the butter and then, over a very low heat, stir in the cream and the lemon zest, adding a little milk if you find the sauce too thick.

Step two In a separate pan, cook the pasta for around 1 minute or until al dente, then drain, and add it to the sauce. Sprinkle with the lemon juice and Parmesan and add salt and pepper to taste. Toss well and distribute onto warm plates. Garnish each serving with a sprig of parsley, if you like.

Pasta for All Seasons

This is a dish for special occasions, and can be eaten warm or cold. It contains truffle oil, which is a very sophisticated and, unfortunately, expensive item.

Step one Wipe the shiitake, oyster and chanterelle mushrooms with a damp cloth and cut away the tough part of the stalks of the shiitake mushrooms. Cut the oyster and shiitake mushrooms into fine strips or use whole if they are small. Heat 4 tablespoons of the oil and fry the oyster and shiitake mushrooms. Add the chanterelles after a few minutes, then cook for another few minutes. Add the garlic, parsley, salt and pepper and fry for a further few minutes, then add the lemon juice. Mix well and set aside.

Step two Cook the pasta for 8–9 minutes or until slightly softer than al dente. Drain and mix in a bowl with the mushroom mixture and ham, and add the cream if eating warm. Sprinkle with truffle oil just before serving. Slices of truffle added to this dish make it very, very special.

Fresh shiitake and oyster mushrooms are now available everywhere because they are cultivated. There is little point in buying them dried. Chanterelles only grow in the wild and they are in season in the spring. They are very expensive and you can't afford to experiment with them, so I suggest you follow a recipe, rather than improvising with them.

Serves 4

150g (5oz) shiitake mushrooms

150g (5oz) oyster mushrooms

100g (4oz) chanterelles

6 tbsp olive oil

1 garlic clove, finely chopped

2 tbsp finely chopped parsley

juice of 1 lemon

300g (11oz) dried fusilli

150g (5oz) smoked ham, cut into small strips

3 tbsp double cream (if eating the dish warm)

2 tbsp truffle oil and/or truffle, finely sliced

salt and freshly ground black pepper

Penne with Chilli Sauce

A fantastic dish for a quick meal on the run, this fiery sauce takes only moments to cook. If you want a milder meal, remove the seeds from the chillies when you chop them.

Serves 4

6 tbsp olive oil

2 garlic cloves, finely chopped

2 red chilli peppers, finely chopped

1 x 400g (14oz) tin chopped tomatoes or 450g (1lb) passata

2 tbsp finely chopped flat-leaf parsley

375g (13oz) dried penne or penne rigate

salt

Step one Heat the oil and briefly fry the garlic and the chillies. Add the tomatoes and cook for a few minutes, then add the parsley and salt to taste.

Step two Cook the pasta in boiling salted water according to the packet instructions or until al dente, then drain. Add the pasta to the sauce and toss together.

Have you made this recipe? Tell us what you think at
www.mykitchentable.co.uk/blog

Springtime Tagliolini

This is my own variation on the famous pesto sauce. It is a lovely dish to greet springtime with, when the desire for the fresh taste of herbs seems to intensify. Try to cook the sauce by substituting, omitting or adding different herbs to suit your personal taste – but include at least five. Rather than blend all the herbs to a paste, I prefer to chop them very finely by hand to give a little texture to the sauce. If you want to substitute dried pasta for the fresh, choose *lingue di passero*.

Step one Melt the butter, add the garlic and gently heat it through – do not fry it. Add the herbs, hazelnuts, lemon zest and half the Parmesan. Now stir in the oil, salt and pepper.

Step two Cook the pasta for 1 minute or until al dente (or according to the packet instructions, if using dried), drain and toss it in the sauce. Add a little of the cooking water if the mixture is too dry. Serve sprinkled with the remaining Parmesan.

Serves 4

75g (3oz) butter

1 garlic clove, peeled and very finely chopped

8 tbsp finely chopped mixed fresh herbs, e.g. basil, mint, coriander, dill, chervil, parsley, chives

1 tbsp finely chopped sage or rosemary or oregano

25g (1oz) shelled hazelnuts, toasted

finely grated zest of ½ lemon

75g (3oz) freshly grated Parmesan

4 tbsp olive oil

450g (1lb) fresh tagliolini or tagliatelle (or see above)

salt and freshly ground black pepper

Tajarin with Butter and Truffle

This is perhaps the quickest and easiest pasta recipe of all, but I am afraid it is also the most expensive! Truffle, especially the white variety from Alba, is one of the most sought-after delicacies, and one of the dearest. It is almost unnecessary to say that to celebrate the most appreciated and sophisticated dish from Piedmont, where I come from, it is absolutely essential to have freshly made tagliolini, or *tajarin* as they are called there.

Serves 4

450g (1lb) fresh tagliolini or tagliatelle (see page 7)

50g (2oz) unsalted butter, roughly chopped

3 tbsp double cream

75g (3oz) freshly grated Parmesan

50–65g (2–2½ oz) white Alba truffle, very finely sliced

salt and freshly ground black pepper

Step one Cook the pasta for 1–2 minutes or until al dente. Drain and reserve a little of the cooking water. Toss the pasta in the butter until every strand is coated. Add the cream, salt and pepper, and enough of the reserved water to achieve a smooth consistency. Sprinkle with the Parmesan and toss well. Serve with the fine slices of truffle on top of each portion.

'Straw And Hay' with Courgettes and Pecorino

My version of straw and hay is nothing other than white and green fresh tagliolini cooked together. Many sauces go well with this combination of pasta. Here is one which is simple and tasty at the same time.

Step one Heat the oil and butter, and gently fry the onion and garlic. Add the courgettes with the tomatoes, and continue to fry gently, stirring, until cooked. This takes a good 10–12 minutes. Add the basil.

Step two Cook the pasta for 1 minute or until al dente and drain. Mix the pasta with the sauce. Add some salt and pepper to taste. Serve with plenty of pecorino cheese.

Serves 4

2 tbsp olive oil

50g (2oz) butter

1 onion, peeled and finely chopped

1 garlic clove, peeled and finely chopped

400g (14oz) firm courgettes, cut into matchsticks

2 ripe tomatoes, sliced into small segments

5 basil leaves, chopped

225g (8oz) each of white and green fresh tagliolini or tagliatelle(see page 7)

75g (3oz) freshly grated pecorino cheese

salt and freshly ground black pepper

Farfalle Genoese-style

See page 7 if you want to make your own farfalle, but if you feel a little too lazy or rushed, the alternative is to buy some, although it's worth remembering that the bought variety will be without eggs. The sauce itself is easy to make and quick.

Serves 4

6 tbsp olive oil

1 large onion, peeled and finely chopped

2 x 450g (1lb) cartons or bottles passata or chopped tomatoes

4 basil leaves, shredded

450g (1lb) fresh farfalle (see page 7)

2 eggs, lightly beaten

50g (2oz) freshly grated pecorino cheese

basil leaves, lightly chopped, to garnish

salt and freshly ground black pepper

Step one Heat the oil and fry the onion until it is soft, then add the tomatoes and cook for a further 10 minutes. Add the basil, salt and pepper.

Step two Cook the pasta for 1–2 minutes or until al dente (or according to the packet instructions if using dried) and drain.

Step three Just before serving, gently reheat the sauce, whisking quickly while pouring in the beaten eggs. Do not allow the mixture to boil. When the sauce starts to thicken, remove from the heat. Toss in the pasta and serve with the pecorino cheese and basil.

Trenette with Basil Sauce

Trenette is the name the Genoese give linguine, where this world-famous pesto sauce comes from. There are a few variations on this sauce, the basis of which should always be the very small-leafed variety of basil which is the one that grows on the Italian Riviera. The only thing that is indispensable in making a good pesto is a pestle and mortar. You can always produce a little more pesto than is needed this time, and keep it in an airtight container in the fridge for up to a week.

Step one Put the garlic, basil and the pine kernels in a mortar. Add the salt. With the pestle, and trying to grind rather than pound the ingredients, use the coarseness of the salt to break down the ingredients. Gradually add the Parmesan or pecorino cheese and continue to work the ingredients into a pulp. Now, very slowly, add a stream of oil and, using the pestle, incorporate just enough oil to obtain a smooth green sauce.

Step two Cook the pasta according to the packet instructions or until al dente, and drain. Toss with the pesto and serve straight away.

Serves 4

2 garlic cloves, peeled and roughly chopped

40g (1½ oz) basil leaves

25g (1oz) pine kernels

½ tsp coarse sea salt

75g (3oz) freshly grated Parmesan or mature pecorino cheese

6 tbsp olive oil

375g (13oz) dried *trenette* (linguine)

Cart Drivers' Spaghetti

Together with pizza, spaghetti is the symbol of Naples. To celebrate artisan spaghetti, here is a curious recipe that not only the Neapolitans but also the Sicilians and Romans claim as their own. The Neapolitan version is very simple and is named in honour of the cart drivers who used to deliver food and wine to big cities. I find the combination of porcini and tuna quite intriguing.

Serves 4

25g (1oz) dried porcini mushrooms

4 tbsp olive oil

1 garlic clove, crushed

50g (2oz) pancetta, finely chopped

200g (7oz) tin tuna in oil, drained

600g (1lb 5oz) *pomodorini* (very sweet cherry tomatoes), chopped, or 500g (1lb 2oz) passata or chopped tomatoes

400g (14oz) spaghetti (fresh or dried)

freshly grated Parmesan, to serve (optional)

salt

freshly ground black pepper (optional)

Step one Soak the porcini in warm water for 30 minutes, then drain and chop, reserving the soaking liquid. Heat the oil in a frying pan, add the garlic and fry gently until softened. Add the pancetta and allow to brown a little. Stir in the porcini and tuna and fry for a few minutes, then add the tomatoes and some salt and simmer for 20 minutes. Stir in a few spoonfuls of the mushroom soaking liquid, just to flavour the sauce, and cook for about 5 minutes longer.

Step two Cook the spaghetti in a large pan of boiling salted water according to the packet instructions or until al dente, then drain and mix with the sauce. Season with black pepper and sprinkle with Parmesan, if liked.

Sardinian Gnocchi with Tomato Sauce

This pasta is still made by hand in Sardinia, using durum wheat flour, saffron and water. It is also manufactured commercially now, but purists say the quality is inferior. If you want to make it yourself, take 350g (12oz) durum wheat flour, a pinch of salt and a sachet of good Sardinian saffron diluted in a cup of warm water. Mix to a fairly stiff dough and then knead for at least half an hour. Take a little of the dough, roll it into a very thin baton and cut it into small pellets. Roll the pasta pellets on a ridged piece of wood, rather like the tool for making butter curls. The result is mini gnocchi, which have to be dried out a little before use. It is easier to buy them ready made!

Step one Heat the oil in a pan, add the onion and fry gently until softened. Add the tomatoes and cook gently for 20 minutes. Towards the end of the cooking time, add the basil leaves and some salt and pepper, plus a little water if the sauce is too thick.

Step two Cook the pasta in a large pan of boiling salted water according to the packet instructions or until al dente (about 11–12 minutes), then drain. Mix in the sauce and serve with the grated pecorino cheese.

Serves 4

5 tbsp extra-virgin olive oil

1 small onion, finely chopped

675g (1½lb) *pomodorini* (very sweet cherry tomatoes), passata or chopped tomatoes

6 basil leaves

400g (14oz) *malloreddus* pasta

50g (2oz) aged pecorino cheese, grated

salt and freshly ground black pepper

Risotto with Two Artichokes

The combination of the two artichokes gives this risotto an extremely delicate flavour. It is suitable for anything from a *piatto unico* (one-course meal) to one of the courses for an elegant dinner party.

Serves 4

4 x 50g (2oz) small globe artichokes (trimmed weight) or hearts from 4 large fresh globe artichokes

600ml (1 pint) chicken or vegetable stock or a bouillon cube

1 small onion, finely chopped

4 tbsp extra-virgin olive oil

100g (4oz) unsalted butter

320g (11½ oz) Jerusalem artichokes, peeled, thinly sliced

350g (12oz) risotto rice (carnaroli, *vialone nano* or arborio)

50g (2oz) freshly grated Parmesan

2 tsp finely chopped flat-leaf parsley

salt and freshly ground black pepper

Step one Cut each small globe artichoke, or the artichoke hearts, in half and slice thinly. Bring the stock to the boil.

Step two In a separate pan, fry the onion gently in the oil and 65g (2½ oz) of the butter until soft but without colouring. Add the globe and Jerusalem artichokes and lightly brown over a moderate heat. Add a little stock and braise for 2 minutes. Add the risotto rice and stir until each grain is coated. Gradually add the stock until it is absorbed and the grains are soft but still have a bite to them. Off the heat, stir in the Parmesan, the remaining butter and the parsley. Check the seasoning and serve.

Pasta Salad Al Fresco

This simple dish is just what you need on a hot, sunny day.

Step one Heat the oil, add the garlic and fry until softened but not browned. Add the tomatoes, basil, and salt and pepper to taste, cover and cook for 10 minutes.

Step two Cook the pasta for 8–9 minutes or until slightly softer than al dente, and drain. Mix with the sauce and eat at room temperature, garnished with the basil.

Serves 4

4 tbsp virgin olive oil

1 garlic clove, peeled and finely chopped

1 x 400g (14oz) tin chopped tomatoes

2 tbsp finely chopped basil leaves

300g (11oz) dried *tubetti lisci*, macaroni or penne

basil leaves, torn, to garnish (optional)

salt and freshly ground black pepper

Chicken Soup with Tagliolini

One doesn't need to be a gastronomic genius to create a recipe like this, but, as often happens, by experimenting and testing one recipe, another comes out as a by-product. After I tested a recipe based on chicken breast, I put the rest of the chicken in water to be boiled for the cat. I went to the garden, collected a few leaves of lovage, a herb similar in flavour to celery but much more scented, and a handful of flat-leaf parsley. I cheated a little by adding a chicken stock cube, but the revelation was the lovage, which gave so much flavour to the stock that it had to be discarded after a short part of the cooking time. With the addition of the pieces of boiled chicken I, not the cat, had a wonderful meal!

Serves 4

450g (1lb) chicken bones, with some meat on them

1.5 litres (2½ pints) water

1 chicken stock cube

150g (5oz) dried or 250g (9oz) fresh tagliolini or tagliatelli (see page 7)

2 lovage leaves

75g (3oz) freshly grated Parmesan

2 tbsp chopped flat-leaf parsley

salt

Step one Put the chicken bones and the water in a large pan with the stock cube, cover and simmer for 1 hour. (You can do this in advance.) Remove the bones, strain the stock, and cut the cooked meat off the bones and into small slivers. Discard the bones.

Step two Return the stock to a clean pan, bring to the boil, add the pasta, the lovage and the chicken slivers. Allow to simmer for 2 minutes, then discard the lovage. Check and continue cooking the pasta until soft, and add salt if necessary. Serve sprinkled with the Parmesan and parsley. Because of the difficulty of eating this dish, the usually forbidden act of using a fork and spoon is allowed!

Pappardelle with Meat Sauce

Pappardelle is a very satisfying pasta indeed, especially when it is accompanied by a meat sauce. This pasta is eaten in Italy whenever a roast is made, with the meat sediment from the roasting tin forming the basis of the sauce. In this recipe I have given you a quicker version.

Step one Heat the oil and gently fry the onion, celery and carrot until soft. Add the pork and beef, and continue frying until the meat is browned. Pour in the wine and let it evaporate for 1–2 minutes. Add the tomato purée with the water, and the bay leaves. Cook for another 10 minutes. Stir in the stock, add salt and pepper to taste, and heat through for 1–2 minutes. Remove the bay leaves.

Step two Cook the pasta for 5–7 minutes or until al dente. Drain and serve with the meat sauce, and sprinkle with a little of the grated Parmesan.

Serves 4

6 tbsp olive oil

1 small onion, peeled and finely chopped

1 celery stick, finely chopped

1 carrot, peeled and finely chopped

200g (7oz) minced pork (or use skinned 100 per cent pork sausages)

200g (7oz) lean minced beef

150ml (5fl oz) dry red wine

3 tbsp tomato purée diluted with 2 tbsp warm water

2 bay leaves

150ml (5fl oz) stock

450g (1lb) pappardelle (fresh or dried)

75g (3oz) freshly grated Parmesan

salt and freshly ground black pepper

For more recipes from My Kitchen Table, sign up for our newsletter at www.mykitchentable.co.uk/newsletter

Pasta Salad with Meat

Ideally some leftovers of roast duck or turkey would do very nicely here, but you can use roast beef or chicken instead.

Serves 4

300g (11oz) dried *pennette lisce* or fusilli

100g (4oz) smoked lean bacon, rinded and cut into pieces

6 tbsp virgin olive oil

2 tbsp tarragon vinegar or white wine vinegar

200g (7oz) roast duck (preferably breast), cut into strips

100g (4oz) mozzarella cheese, cut into narrow strips

100g (4oz) lean Parma ham

1–2 tbsp finely chopped flat-leaf parsley

2 tbsp finely chopped spring onions

2 large gherkins, pickled with dill, cut into matchsticks

1 tbsp creamed horseradish

few drops Tabasco sauce

salt and freshly ground black pepper

Step one Cook the pasta for 7 minutes or until slightly softer than al dente. Drain and allow to cool.

Step two Fry the bacon in its own fat until crispy, then drain on paper towels.

Step three Put the oil, vinegar, salt and pepper in a bowl and mix well. Add all the other ingredients and mix together well with the pasta. Taste again for seasoning. Serve cold.

Bucatini with Bacon, Cheese and Eggs

I don't believe this sauce needs any introduction. It is well-known in Britain, although it is not always made as it should be! The eggs must not be cooked and it is this that gives the character to the sauce. In some variations on this version, double cream is added too, but I think it then becomes too rich, although I leave this up to you. Bucatini are also known as *perciatelli*, and are like spaghetti, but with a hollow centre.

Step one Cook the pasta for 7–8 minutes or until al dente, then drain it.

Step two Heat the butter or oil and fry the pancetta or bacon until lightly browned, and set aside. Lightly beat the egg yolks and the milk in a bowl and add the pecorino cheese. Pour the egg mixture into the bacon and add the pasta. Toss the hot pasta to coat it with the uncooked egg, which will set slightly on the pasta. Add plenty of black pepper.

Caution *This recipe contains lightly cooked eggs.*

Serves 4

400g (14oz) dried bucatini or spaghetti

50g (2oz) butter or 6 tbsp olive oil

100g (4oz) pancetta or bacon, rinded and cut into small strips

4 egg yolks

1 tbsp milk

40g (1½ oz) freshly grated mature pecorino cheese

freshly ground black pepper

Rigatoni with Pork Ragout

Rigatoni is another pasta which is very much loved in the south of Italy, where some people have it with hardly any sauce so they are able to taste the pasta itself. A good ragout should cook for at least 1 hour. I remember my grandmother starting to prepare this sauce in the morning and letting it bubble away, just like hot volcanic lava, she used to say, until it was ready for lunch. By the way, the meat tastes heavenly at the end of the cooking. In Italy we would enjoy this dish with some vegetables as our main course.

Serves 4

8 tbsp olive oil

400g (14oz) pork with bone, e.g. neck, shoulder chops or spare ribs

1 onion, peeled and finely sliced

150ml (5fl oz) dry white wine

2 x 400g (14oz) cartons or bottles passata or chopped tomatoes

2 tbsp tomato purée

2 basil leaves, shredded

375g (13oz) dried rigatoni

75g (3oz) freshly grated Parmesan

salt and freshly ground black pepper

Step one Heat the oil in a heavy-based saucepan, add the meat and fry for several minutes until browned. Add the onion and fry until golden. Pour in the wine and let the alcohol evaporate for 2 minutes. Add the tomatoes and the tomato purée, cover and simmer very gently for 30 minutes. Stir from time to time. Add the basil, salt and black pepper to taste, and cook for another 30 minutes. If the sauce becomes too dry add a little water.

Step two Cook the pasta for 8–9 minutes or until al dente, and drain. Mix the pasta with some of the sauce and serve with the remaining sauce and the Parmesan.

Orecchiette with Lamb Ragout

This is a similar sauce to the basic ragu or Bolognese sauce, only it contains more meat. Try to use neck cutlets of lamb for this sauce because they give it a fine flavour, and are ideal as a main course, after or alongside the pasta. *Orecchiette baresi* are so called because they are originally from Bari, in Puglia.

Step one Heat the oil in a heavy-based pan and fry the lamb cutlets on both sides until browned. Add the onion and fry until soft. Add the wine and continue cooking for 2–3 minutes. Stir in the tomatoes and tomato purée, cover and simmer very gently for about 1 hour. Stir from time to time. If the sauce becomes too dry, add a little water. Add salt and pepper to taste.

Step two Cook the pasta for 12–14 minutes or until al dente, and drain. Mix with the sauce. Serve sprinkled with a little of the pecorino cheese.

Serves 4

2 tbsp olive oil

550g (1¼ lb) neck cutlets of lamb

1 onion, peeled and finely sliced

150ml (5fl oz) dry white wine

2 x 400g (14oz) cartons or bottles passata or chopped tomatoes

1 tbsp tomato purée

400g (14oz) dried *orecchiette baresi* or conchiglie

75g (3oz) freshly grated pecorino cheese

salt and freshly ground black pepper

Ziti Neapolitan-style

This recipe takes some time and patience, but the result makes it worthwhile. Let me show you how my mother taught me to cook it.

Serves 8

for the meatballs

1 garlic clove

1 tbsp parsley

40g (1½ oz) fresh breadcrumbs

milk, for soaking

300g (11oz) minced beef

25g (1oz) freshly grated Parmesan

2 eggs

salt and freshly ground black pepper

oil, for frying

for the sauce

1 onion

5 basil leaves

4 tbsp olive oil

100g (4oz) chicken livers, chopped

2 x 400g (14oz) tins chopped tomatoes

for the layers

450g (1lb) dried *ziti* or penne

100g (4oz) spicy Neapolitan salami

350g (12oz) fontina or mozzarella cheese

4 eggs, lightly beaten

75g (3oz) freshly grated Parmesan

Step one Preheat the oven to 200°C/400°F/gas 6. To make the meatballs, first peel and chop the garlic, chop the parsely and soak the breadcrumbs in a little milk for 5 minutes, then squeeze them dry. Mix together the minced beef, the garlic, parsley, Parmesan, and breadcrumbs in a bowl. Lightly beat the eggs and add them to the bowl along with a little salt and pepper and mix thoroughly. Use your hands to shape the mixture into walnut-sized meatballs. Heat a little oil in a frying pan and fry the meatballs in batches for about 3 minutes until browned on all sides. Remove and drain on kitchen paper.

Step two To make the sauce, peel and chop the onion and shred the basil leaves, then heat the oil in a clean pan and fry the onion until nearly transparent. Add the chicken livers and cook for another 3 minutes. Stir in the tomatoes, cover and simmer for 20 minutes over a low heat. Add the basil and a little salt and pepper, if you like, and simmer for another 10 minutes.

Step three Cook the pasta for 5–7 minutes or until al dente, and drain. Toss with some of the sauce, so that the pasta is coated.

Step four Lightly butter a 20 x 25cm (8 x 10in) baking dish with sides 7.5cm (3in) deep. Spread a layer of sauce over the bottom then add a layer of pasta. Slice and arrange some salami, some of the meatballs and slices of fontina or mozzarella cheese on top. Repeat this sequence until you reach the final layer of cheese, then pour on the beaten eggs which will bind the pasta together. Finish with a layer of sauce and the Parmesan. Bake for 25 minutes. When it is cooked let the dish stand for 5 minutes before dividing it into portions with a knife and serving.

Amatrice-style Bucatini

This Abruzzese recipe is typical of Amatrice, the farming town it comes from. It is also eaten a lot in Rome as Amatrice is on the border of Lazio. It is a classic in the Italian pasta repertoire.

Step one Heat the oil and fry the pancetta or bacon, the onion and the chilli for 3–4 minutes until slightly brown. Add the tomatoes, cover and cook gently for 10–15 minutes.

Step two Cook the pasta for 7–8 minutes or until al dente, and drain. Toss in the sauce, and serve sprinkled with the grated pecorino cheese.

Serves 4

3 tbsp olive oil

150g (5oz) pancetta or bacon, rinded and cut into strips

1 small onion, peeled and finely chopped

1 small chilli pepper, finely chopped

1 x 450g (1lb) carton or bottle passata or chopped tomatoes

375g (13oz) dried bucatini or spaghetti

50g (2oz) freshly grated pecorino cheese

Marille with Peas

The *marille* used for this recipe was the original 'designer pasta'. It was designed by Giugiaro, the famous Italian car designer, on behalf of one of the leading pasta manufacturers. But engaging Giugiaro was not just a publicity gag: *marille*'s ribbed tubular shape held a large amount of sauce, the ultimate aim of the best pasta. So it is very sad that the production of *marille* has been discontinued. As an alternative, I suggest you use large *gomiti* or rigatoni.

Serves 4

50g (2oz) butter

150g (5oz) smoked bacon, rinded and cut into strips

1 x 450g (1lb) carton or bottle passata or chopped tomatoes, or 4 large ripe tomatoes, skinned and de-seeded

200g (7oz) frozen petits pois or small fresh peas

375g (13oz) *marille*, *gomiti* or rigatoni (fresh or dried)

8 basil leaves, shredded

150g (5oz) mascarpone cheese

75g (3oz) freshly grated Parmesan

salt and freshly ground black pepper

Step one Heat the butter and fry the bacon until crisp. Add the tomatoes and the petits pois or fresh peas, and cook for 5 minutes (or cover and cook for 15 minutes if using fresh peas).

Step two Cook the pasta for 10–12 minutes or until al dente. Add the basil leaves and mascarpone cheese to the sauce and stir until just warmed through and the cheese has melted. Add salt and pepper to taste. Drain the pasta and add to the sauce. Mix well with the Parmesan.

Rigatoni with Rich Bolognese Sauce

You can prepare this wonderful dish a day in advance, let it set for twenty-four hours and bake it at the last minute.

Step one Preheat the oven to 220°C/425°C/gas 7. If using dried ceps, soak them in warm water for 20 minutes. Drain the ceps and squeeze dry, then roughly chop them. Put the sweetbreads in boiling water and blanch for 10 minutes. Strain and remove the skin and nerves. Slice the sweetbreads and fresh ceps or button mushrooms (depending on which you are using).

Step two To make the meat sauce, begin by chopping the onion and chicken livers, then thickly slicing the Parma ham and cutting it into strips. Heat the oil in a large, heavy-based pan and fry the onion for 1 minute. Add the chicken livers, minced chicken or veal and Parma ham, and fry for another few minutes. Add the sweetbreads and continue to fry until everything is lightly browned. Add the fresh ceps, or the button mushrooms and dried ceps, to the pan, with the Marsala wine. Simmer gently for about 2 minutes, then stir in the tomatoes. Cover and simmer the sauce very gently for 2 hours, stirring from time to time. Taste and add salt and pepper, if you like.

Step three To make the white sauce, bring the milk to the boil in a saucepan. In a separate pan, melt the butter and stir in the flour. Cook the butter and flour for 1 minute over a moderate heat, stirring continuously, to make a roux. Reduce the heat and gradually stir in the milk until the sauce has thickened. Add salt and nutmeg to taste and set aside.

Step four Cook the pasta for just 4 minutes, and drain. Toss in a little of the white sauce to prevent the pasta shapes from sticking together.

Step five Lightly butter an 20 x 25cm (8 x 10in) baking dish with sides about 7.5cm (3 in) deep. Put a layer of pasta in the dish, then add one-third of the meat sauce, followed by one-third of the white sauce. Sprinkle with Parmesan. Repeat this sequence twice more, finishing with Parmesan cheese. Bake for 40 minutes.

Serves 5–6

For the meat sauce

200g (7oz) fresh ceps, or 200g (7oz) button mushrooms together with 20g (¾oz) dried ceps

150g (5oz) veal sweetbreads

1 onion

200g (7oz) chicken livers

6 tbsp olive oil

100g (4oz) lean Parma ham

200g (7oz) chicken breasts or veal, coarsely minced

150ml (5fl oz) dry Marsala wine

3 x 450g (1lb) cartons or bottles passata or chopped tomatoes

For the white sauce

1 litre (1¾ pts) milk

50g (2oz) butter

2 tbsp plain flour

freshly grated nutmeg

For the layers

450g (1lb) dried rigatoni

150g (5oz) freshly grated Parmesan

Tagliatelle with Radicchio and Rocket

The bitterness and the sharpness of rocket gives quite a sophisticated taste to this pasta, which, when combined with the speck, reminds me of the style of cooking in north-east Italy.

Serves 4

4 tbsp olive oil

1 red onion, peeled and roughly chopped

100g (4oz) speck, rinded and cut into small strips

2 tbsp dry red wine

150g (5oz) radicchio, finely chopped

450g (1lb) fresh tagliatelle (see page 7)

100g (4oz) rocket, roughly chopped

salt and freshly ground black pepper

Step one Heat the oil and gently fry the onion and the speck, until the onion is soft. Pour in the wine and let it evaporate for 1–2 minutes. Now add the radicchio, and allow it to soften. Add salt and pepper.

Step two Cook the pasta for 3–5 minutes or until al dente. Drain and mix with the sauce. Serve sprinkled with the rocket.

Tagliatelle with Chicken Livers

Chicken livers are very much part of many Italian sauces, and in this dish they predominate. Extremely easy to prepare, this is a particularly tasty recipe.

Step one Cut the chicken livers into small slivers. Heat the oil and fry the onion very gently for 5 minutes. Add the chicken livers and bay leaves, and fry gently for another 6 minutes over a low heat. Add the nutmeg and sherry, and let the alcohol evaporate for around 1–2 minutes. Stir in the tomato purée and enough stock or water to bring the sauce to a smooth consistency. Add salt and pepper to taste.

Step two Meanwhile, cook the pasta for 3–5 minutes or until al dente. Drain and toss well in the sauce. Serve sprinkled with the pecorino cheese.

Serves 4

300g (11oz) chicken livers, trimmed

6 tbsp olive oil

1 large onion, peeled and very finely sliced

4 bay leaves

pinch of nutmeg

3 tbsp dry sherry

2 tbsp tomato purée

about 2 tbsp stock or water

450g (1lb) fresh tagliatelle (see page 7)

75g (3oz) freshly grated pecorino cheese

salt and freshly ground black pepper

Have you made this recipe? Tell us what you think at
www.mykitchentable.co.uk/blog

Orecchiette with Broccoli and Ham

The purists of Puglian cuisine will be horrified at my audacity in adding ham to the classic dish *orecchiette con cime di rape* and substituting broccoli for turnip tops. However, I find it an extremely good combination and still in keeping with the region.

Serves 4

6 tbsp olive oil

50g (2oz) prosciutto, cut into small cubes

1 garlic clove, finely chopped

⅓ chilli pepper, finely chopped

6 small cherry tomatoes, quartered

200g (7oz) broccoli florets

2 tbsp finely chopped flat-leaf parsley

400g (14oz) orecchiette or conchiglie (fresh or dried)

40g (1½oz) pecorino cheese, grated (optional)

salt and freshly ground black pepper

Step one Heat the oil in a pan, add the prosciutto and fry for a few minutes. Add the garlic, chilli and tomatoes and fry briefly, then stir in the broccoli florets and a little water. Cover the pan and cook gently until the broccoli is tender, then stir in the parsley.

Step two Cook the pasta in a large pan of lightly salted boiling water for 12–15 minutes, according to the packet instructions or until al dente. Drain and add to the sauce. Mix well and season with salt and pepper. Serve with the pecorino cheese, if desired.

Tagliolini with Veal

This is a more substantial dish in which the veal can be replaced with chicken breast for a similar, but cheaper, dish. It is an almost instant meal because the meat cooks in such a short time.

Step one Cut the meat into very fine strips. Heat the oil and fry the onion until transparent. Add the meat and fry for 5–7 minutes until browned and cooked through. Pour in the wine and let it evaporate for 1–2 minutes. Add the sage and salt and pepper to taste.

Step two Cook the pasta for 1–2 minutes or until al dente. Drain and reserve 1 tablespoon of cooking water to moisten the sauce. Stir the pasta into the sauce with the reserved water, and heat through. Sprinkle with the Parmesan and toss well.

Serves 4

250g (9oz) lean veal

6 tbsp olive oil

1 onion, peeled and finely chopped

3 tbsp dry white wine

8 leaves sage, roughly chopped

450g (1lb) fresh tagliolini or tagliatelle (see page 7)

75g (3oz) freshly grated Parmesan

salt and freshly ground black pepper

For a video masterclass on making fresh pasta, go to www.mykitchentable.co.uk/videos/freshpasta

Pappardelle with Quail Sauce

I tried to discover where pappardelle comes from without success. It is the widest pasta, and extremely satisfying. In this dish the combination of quail and morels is wonderful. If you don't feel altogether confident about boning the quail yourself ask if your butcher will do it for you.

Serves 4

25g (1oz) dried morels

50g (2oz) butter

1 celery stick, very finely sliced

breasts and livers of 4 quails, finely sliced

150ml (5fl oz) dry red wine

4 tbsp double cream (optional)

375g (13oz) dried egg pappardelle

75g (3oz) freshly grated Parmesan

salt and freshly ground black pepper

Step one Soak the morels in warm water for 20 minutes or until soft. Drain and squeeze them dry, retaining the strained soaking liquid. Slice the larger mushrooms and leave the smaller ones whole. Heat the butter and gently fry the celery. When softened add the sliced quail and livers, and fry for a few minutes. Add the morels and stir in the wine. Let the wine evaporate for 2–3 minutes. Stir in 2–3 tablespoons of the reserved soaking liquid and cook for another few minutes. Add salt and pepper to taste. If you prefer a richer sauce, stir in the cream.

Step two Cook the pasta for about 6 minutes or until al dente, and drain. Toss with the sauce, and mix well, adding the Parmesan.

Risotto with Lentils and Sausages

This dish is produced in various ways and is typical of the Vercelli area and Novara, the main commercial centre of Italian rice cultivation. Traditionally, you would use rice from the last harvest and the first sausage made with a newly killed pig. This is a one-course meal, the quantity is abundant and it is a dish to enjoy on a day when you are really hungry. If you do not have lentils, you can use beans or chickpeas as a substitute.

Step one Simmer the lentils, *salamini* and bay leaf in the stock for 15 minutes, covered.

Step two Finely chop the onion, then peel the carrots and cut them along with the celery into 5mm (¼in) dice. Fry the onion gently in the oil until soft, but without colouring. Add the potatoes, celery, carrots and tomatoes and fry gently for 2 minutes. Add the risotto rice and stir to coat each grain. Stir in 1 ladleful of broth, lentils and sausages to the rice at a time, and continue to stir, allowing each ladleful to be absorbed into the rice grains before more is added. Continue until all is incorporated, when the rice should be creamy, but still retain some bite. Check the seasoning and serve.

Serves 4

200g (7oz) green lentils

400g (14oz) *salamini* (a type of *luganiga* – Italian sausage)

1 bay leaf

2.25 litres (4 pints) chicken stock or a bouillon cube

1 small onion

2 carrots

2 sticks celery

5 tbsp extra-virgin olive oil

200g (7oz) potatoes, peeled and cut into 5mm (¼in) dice

2 ripe tomatoes, chopped, or 2 tbsp passata or chopped tomatoes

320g (11½oz) risotto rice (carnaroli, *vialone nano* or arborio)

salt and freshly ground black pepper

Tortellini in Puff Pastry

The idea of putting pasta in a pastry case is to collect all the aromas and to release them all at once in front of guests. One could also say it is a good piece of culinary showmanship! In any case, the effect on your guests will be to elicit surprise and admiration.

Serves 4

400g (14oz) puff pastry, thawed if frozen

40g (1½oz) butter, plus extra for greasing

1 shallot, finely chopped

100g (4oz) cooked smoked ham, sliced

4 sage leaves

freshly grated nutmeg

400g (14oz) fresh, meat-filled tortellini

200ml (7fl oz) single cream

75g (3oz) freshly grated Parmesan

salt and freshly ground black pepper

milk, for glazing

Step one Preheat the oven to 220°C/425°F/gas 7. Thinly roll out the pastry on a lightly floured surface until it is large enough to cover the back of an oval ovenproof dish roughy 23 x 18cm (9 x 7in) and 7.5cm (3in) deep, plus allow an extra 7.5cm (3in) all round. Cut the pastry out around the dish. Re-roll trimmings, if necessary, and cut out a lid that is slightly larger than the base of the dish.

Step two Lightly butter the back of the dish and, with the help of the rolling pin, lay the larger piece of pastry over. Trim the edge to neaten. Lightly butter a baking sheet and place the pastry lid on it. Bake both base and lid for 25–30 minutes until golden. Cool slightly, then remove the pastry base and place in an ovenproof serving dish.

Step three Heat the butter in a pan and briefly fry the shallot for 1 minute to soften slightly. Add the ham, sage and nutmeg to taste and fry for 2 minutes, stirring.

Step four Meanwhile, cook the pasta for 3 minutes, or according to the packet instructions, and drain. Add the cream, Parmesan and pasta to the ham mixture and mix together well. Add seasoning to taste. Pour the mixture into the pastry base. Cover tightly with the pastry lid and glaze with milk. Bake for 5 minutes to reheat the pastry, then serve at once.

Sage is one of five herbs that are all-important in Italian cookery, and although I always prefer to use it fresh, I admit that the dried variety still has a natural aroma when cooked. If you are using dried ground sage, use only ¼–½ teaspoon.

Spaghetti in the Square

You need an appointment with certain fishermen in Sicily to go fishing at night with a *lampara* – a huge light positioned on the bow of the boat in order to scrutinise the shallows. I was taken out in a small boat by two fishermen armed with harpoons. The sea should have been as smooth as oil, but instead it was very rough, and all we managed to catch was an octopus and a scorpion fish. I had to improvise with them and this is the dish I cooked in the piazza for the fishermen. They enjoyed it, despite the meagre ingredients. Octopus is easily available; the scorpion fish can be replaced with pieces of monkfish, if you have trouble finding it.

Step one Clean the octopus, removing the eyes and beak. Heat the oil in a large pan, add the octopus, scorpion fish, garlic, chilli and tomatoes, then cover and cook on a gentle heat for 20 minutes. Remove the scorpion fish and octopus from the pan. Bone the scorpion fish and flake the flesh. Cut the octopus into chunks. Put the flesh of both back in the pan, add the wine and some salt and continue to cook slowly for 15–20 minutes, or until the octopus is tender. Add some water if the sauce gets too thick.

Step two Cook the spaghetti in a large pan of boiling salted water until al dente, then drain and mix with the sauce. Sprinkle with the parsley and serve.

Serves 4

1 x 1kg (2¼ lb) octopus

6 tbsp virgin olive oil

1 x 300g (11oz) scorpion fish, cleaned

1 garlic clove, finely chopped

1 small chilli pepper, finely chopped

800g (1¾lb) passata or chopped tomatoes

100ml (3½ fl oz) dry white wine

500g (1lb 2oz) spaghetti (fresh or dried)

2 tbsp coarsely chopped flat-leaf parsley

salt

Macaroni with Sardines

Don't cook this recipe unless you find very fresh sardines. I once ate this typical Sicilian speciality in an Italian restaurant much praised by a food critic as the best Italian restaurant of the year. I had to send the dish back because the taste and smell of cod liver oil, which is typical of old sardines, were repulsive.

Serves 4

6 anchovy fillets (salted or in oil)

400g (14oz) fresh sardines

1 large fennel bulb

1 sachet saffron powder or a pinch of saffron strands

6 tbsp olive oil

1 onion, peeled and finely chopped

40g (1½ oz) raisins

25g (1oz) pine kernels

375g (13oz) dried macaroni or bucatini

salt and freshly ground black pepper

Step one If using salted anchovies, soak them in water for 30 minutes. Dry the anchovies on kitchen paper and remove any large bones. Remove the sardine heads and tails, and slit the sardines open along the underside. Clean them thoroughly, removing the black bones.

Step two Trim and cut the fennel into quarters and cook both the bulb and the leaves in slightly salted water for about 15 minutes or until tender. Remove the fennel and retain the cooking water. Once the fennel has cooled slightly, roughly chop it. If using saffron strands put them in 2 tablespoons boiling water until the water has coloured.

Step three Heat the oil and fry the onion until golden. Add the anchovies and let them soften. Add the sardines and cook for another few minutes. Stir in the fennel, raisins, pine kernels and saffron powder, or strained soaking liquid. Add salt and pepper to taste, and cook briefly to make a smooth sauce.

Step four Meanwhile, cook the pasta for 7–8 minutes or until al dente, and drain. Toss in the sauce.

Spaghetti for Pinuccia

I created this recipe in honour of Pinuccia, the exceptional chef at the San Giovanni restaurant, in Casarza. I was incredibly impressed by her dedication in producing outstanding food with ingredients hunted personally on a daily basis. If you are in that area, pay her a visit – it will be nicely rewarded. You could use cooked king prawns here if you can't get raw ones and reduce the cooking time slightly. Also, if you use tagliolini, the pasta will take slightly less time to cook.

Step one Peel the central part of the prawns, leaving the head and tail shells intact. Heat the oil in a frying pan and add the garlic, chilli and parsley, taking care not to burn them. Then add the prawns and fry for a minute. Stir in the wine and the tomatoes. Cook for a further 2–3 minutes.

Step two Cook the pasta in slightly salted boiling water. If using fresh, cook for 2–3 minutes; if using the dried variety, about 6–7 minutes. Drain the pasta, add to the pan with the sauce, mix very well and serve immediately, garnished with the chopped basil.

Serves 4

400g (14oz) uncooked king prawns

6 tbsp olive oil

1 garlic clove, chopped

1 medium-sized red chilli pepper, chopped

1 tbsp chopped flat-leaf parsley

5 tbsp white wine

400g (14oz) passata or chopped tomatoes

500g (1¼ lb) spaghetti (fresh or dried) or fresh egg tagliolini

basil, finely chopped, to garnish

Black Angel's Hair with Scallops

I chose the black *capelli d'angelo* for this. Made with the addition of cuttlefish ink to give it its colour, and obtainable from the best Italian food shops, it combines with the very tender scallops to produce a wonderful marriage of taste, colour and texture. It is also an extremely quick recipe, taking just minutes to prepare.

Serves 4

400g (14oz), or
8 large, or 16 small,
fresh scallops, cleaned

6 tbsp virgin olive oil

1 garlic clove, peeled
and finely chopped

1 small red chilli
pepper, finely
chopped

150ml (5fl oz) dry
white wine

2 tbsp finely chopped
parsley

375g (13oz) dried
black *capelli d'angelo*
or spaghetti

salt

Step one If using large scallops, detach the coral and cut the white meat into 4 slices; if using small scallops, leave them whole. Heat the oil and gently fry the garlic, chilli and white meat, with the corals, for 1 minute. Add the wine, parsley and salt to taste.

Step two Cook the pasta for 3–4 minutes, or until al dente, and drain. (This will take slightly longer if using spaghetti.) Add to the scallop mixture, mix well and serve.

Have you made this recipe? Tell us what you think at
www.mykitchentable.co.uk/blog

Tagliolini with Red Mullet

Pinuccia, who cooks in the San Giovanni restaurant in Casarza, was a fishmonger before becoming a fantastic cook and perfectionist, and she knows all the tricks of the trade. And, above all, she never compromises about the freshness of fish. How wonderful to know that you are in the hands of a real professional. The *triglie di scoglio* which were used for the dish I ate there were caught that same morning.

Step one Scale, gut and fillet the fish and cut into 5cm (2in) strips. Heat the oil in a frying pan. Fry the garlic, half the parsley and all the fish. Add the wine, stir well and cook for a couple of minutes. Season with salt and add the tomatoes. Sprinkle with the remaining parsley and cook for a further 2–3 minutes.

Step two Bring a large pan of slightly salted water to the boil. Add the tagliolini. If you are using fresh pasta, cook for about 2–3 minutes; if you are using the dried variety, 6–8 minutes.

Step three When cooked, drain the pasta and add to the sauce. Sauté for a short time on the heat to coat well. Serve the dish immediately.

Serves 4

675g (1½ lb) red mullet

3 tbsp olive oil

1 garlic clove, chopped

1 tbsp chopped flat-leaf parsley

5 tbsp white wine

250g (9oz) passata or chopped tomatoes

500g (1¼ lb) tagliolini or tagliatelle (fresh or dried)

salt

Tagliatelle with Bottarga

This Sardinian speciality, not well known here in England, is based on *bottarga*, which is salted and air-dried roe of grey mullet or tuna fish. *Bottarga* is usually grated over pasta as a flavouring, but can also be eaten in thin slices with lemon and oil as an appetiser. The best *bottarga* for this recipe is the tuna. This is an extremely quick recipe provided you can get hold of the *bottarga*. It is not impossible to find it here, but you'll need the help of a good Italian delicatessen! There is a pre-grated variety in jars which gives quite good results.

Serves 4

4 tbsp virgin olive oil

1 medium onion, peeled and finely chopped

450g (1lb) fresh tagliatelle or spaghetti (see page 7)

1 tbsp chopped flat-leaf parsley

1 tbsp chopped basil

50g (2oz) *bottarga*, grated

Step one Heat the oil and fry the onion until transparent.

Step two Cook the pasta for 3–5 minutes or until al dente, adding only a little salt to the cooking water as the bottarga is itself very salty. Drain the pasta and toss in the olive oil and onion. Add the chopped parsley and basil, and the grated bottarga.

Square Spaghetti with Garlic and Anchovy

This is a recipe of which I am very proud. It is along the lines of *bagna cauda*, that famous garlic and anchovy sauce from Piedmont which is usually eaten as part of an antipasto. The sweetness of the grilled red and yellow peppers contrasts perfectly with the garlic and anchovy. This type of pasta is also called *maccheroni alla chitarra* because it is made using a stringed cutter which resembles a guitar.

Step one Cook the garlic cloves gently in the milk for around 30 minutes until softened. If using salted anchovies, soak them in water for 30 minutes. Dry the anchovies on paper towels and remove any large bones.

Step two Put the peppers under a hot grill until the skins are blackened. Allow to cool slightly, then peel the skin away from the peppers, discard the seeds, and finely slice them. Keep the pepper slices warm.

Step three When the garlic is soft, take the pan off the heat. Add the anchovies and stir with a spoon until dissolved. Pass the milk, garlic and the anchovies through a metal sieve into a pan. Heat gently and add the butter. Do not cook the sauce, just heat it enough to melt the butter. Take the sauce off the heat.

Step four Cook the pasta for 3–5 minutes or until al dente. Drain and toss well with the sauce. Serve the pasta with the slices of pepper on top.

Serves 4

2 whole garlic bulbs, peeled and broken into cloves

300ml (10fl oz) milk

16 anchovy fillets (salted or in oil)

3 peppers (yellow and red)

75g (3oz) butter, roughly chopped

450g (1lb) fresh square spaghetti or spaghetti (see page 7)

Pasta with Lobster

This rather posh-sounding recipe is a very common dish in parts of Italy where lobsters are caught. I think that fishermen are probably the only people to eat this cheaply, because by the time lobsters arrive in the shops they are very expensive. However, you only need one 675g–1kg (1½–2¼lb) lobster to make four servings of this wonderful, simple recipe. *Fidelini* are also known as spaghettini; or linguine will do for this recipe. If you can't get lobster, try using giant prawns.

Serves 4

1 x 675g–1kg (1½–2¼lb) fresh lobster (or cooked giant prawns, shelled and cut into small pieces)

6 tbsp olive oil

1 garlic clove, peeled and finely chopped

675g (1½lb) very ripe tomatoes, skinned, de-seeded and chopped, or 2 x 400g (14oz) tins chopped tomatoes

2 tbsp chopped flat-leaf parsley

2 tbsp dry white wine

400g (14oz) dried *fidelini* or linguine

salt and freshly ground black pepper

Step one If using fresh lobster, bring a large pan of water to the boil. Put the lobster in it and cover with a lid. Simmer over a low heat for 20 minutes. Take out the lobster and leave to cool. Place the lobster on a board and, using a sharp knife, cut along the entire length of its back. Open out the two halves and remove the two gills (towards the head), the dark vein running down the tail, and the small stomach sac in the head. Do not discard the green, creamy liver in the head, as this is delicious. If it's a female lobster you should also retain the coral. Using a small skewer, extract the tail meat. Crack open the large claws and remove the meat, discarding the thin membrane. Cut any larger pieces of meat into smaller pieces.

Step two Heat the oil and gently fry the garlic. Add the tomatoes and the parsley and cook for another 10 minutes. Add the lobster (with any juices) to the sauce with the wine, and add salt and pepper to taste. If using prawns as an alternative to lobster, add them to the sauce at this point. Cook for 1–2 minutes to let the alcohol evaporate and heat the fish.

Step three Cook the pasta for 7–8 minutes or until al dente, and drain. Toss with some of the sauce, and serve with the remaining sauce on top.

Angel's Hair with Crab

This very fine type of pasta is usually sold in cellophane packets. It is extremely fragile and that is why it is only made in nests. When you buy it, you should check that the strands are intact and that you're not taking home a lot of broken pieces. For this recipe you also need very fresh crab meat.

Step one Heat the butter and add the garlic, then the crab meat, stirring for 1 minute. Add the tomatoes. Mix well and cook for another minute. Add salt and plenty of pepper.

Step two Cook the pasta for 2–3 minutes or until al dente, and drain. Mix well with the sauce and serve sprinkled with basil.

Serves 4

50g (2oz) butter

½ garlic clove, peeled and finely chopped

350g (12oz) fresh, cooked, white crab meat

1 x 450g (1lb) carton or bottle passata or chopped tomatoes

375g (13oz) dried *capelli d'angelo* or spaghetti

1 tbsp torn basil

salt and freshly ground black pepper

Fettuccine with Smoked Salmon

This is one of the recipes I created using a typically British ingredient –
smoked salmon. The sauce is very easy to prepare and is well suited to
any of the flat egg pastas.

Serves 4

375g (13oz) dried egg
fettuccine

75g (3oz) butter, cut
into small cubes

250g (9oz) smoked
salmon, cut into strips

2 tbsp finely chopped
dill

salt and freshly ground
black pepper

Step one Cook the pasta for 10–12 minutes or until al dente, and
drain. While still very hot, add the butter, the salmon and the dill.
Taste for salt and add generous amounts of black pepper.

Cavatelli with Mussels

A speciality of Puglia and particularly of Bari, where *cavatelli* are still hand-made for special occasions from hard durum wheat semolina flour and water. You can buy high-quality commercially manufactured *cavatelli* in good delicatessens. As it is quite soupy, this pasta dish may be eaten with a spoon.

Step one Scrub the mussels thoroughly under cold running water, pulling out the beards and discarding any open mussels that do not close when tapped on a work surface. Put the mussels in a large pan with 2 tablespoons of water, cover and cook over a medium–high heat for 3–4 minutes, shaking the pan occasionally, until all the shells are open (discard any that remain closed). Remove the shells from half the mussels. Strain the cooking juices through a very fine sieve and reserve.

Step two Heat the oil in a frying pan, add the garlic and chilli and fry gently until the garlic is softened but not browned. Cut some of the cherry tomatoes in half. Add the halved and the whole tomatoes to the pan and fry until softened. Add the mussels, their cooking juices and the parsley and heat through gently. Season with salt and pepper to taste.

Step three Cook the pasta in a large pan of lightly salted boiling water according to the packet instructions or until al dente. Drain and stir into the mussel sauce. I like to pour a stream of extra-virgin olive oil onto each portion for extra flavour.

Serves 4

1kg (2¼ lb) mussels

6 tbsp extra-virgin olive oil, plus extra to serve

1 garlic clove, finely chopped

1 small chilli pepper, finely diced

300g (11oz) cherry tomatoes

1 small bunch finely chopped flat-leaf parsley

400g (14oz) *cavatelli* or conchiglie (fresh or dried)

salt and freshly ground black pepper

For more recipes from My Kitchen Table, sign up for our newsletter at www.mykitchentable.co.uk/newsletter

Vermicelli with Clam Sauce

In Naples spaghetti are called *vermicelli*, which really means little worms! The clams in this recipe should be the small, grey ones. Alternatively, try the Venus clam which is completely white and very delicious. It is possible to use the tinned variety, but remember most of its flavour disappears in the processing.

Serves 4

450g (1lb) fresh clams in their shells

6 tbsp olive oil

1 garlic clove, peeled and chopped

1 small chilli pepper, finely chopped

1 x 400g (14oz) tin chopped tomatoes

375g (13oz) dried *vermicelli*

1 tbsp finely chopped flat-leaf parsley

salt and freshly ground black pepper

Step one Thoroughly wash the clams. Discard any broken ones and those that appear empty. Put the clams in a large pan with a lid and place over a low heat. Shake them in the pan from time to time until all the clam shells are open. There will be some 'milky' water at the bottom of the pan which should be reserved. Remove the clams and discard most of the shells, keeping some for a garnish.

Step two Heat the oil in a separate pan and fry the garlic and the chilli without letting them brown. Add the tomatoes and cook for another 6–7 minutes. If the sauce needs more liquid, add a little of the reserved cooking liquid. Add the clams and cook for another 1–2 minutes. Taste for salt, remembering that the clam water is already salty. Add a little pepper.

Step three Cook the pasta for 7–8 minutes or until al dente, and drain. Mix with the sauce and serve sprinkled with the parsley.

Sparrow Tongues with Anchovies

Don't worry, the term sparrow tongues is only the translation of the name of a type of pasta and nothing to do with a banquet of a Roman emperor! This type of flat spaghetti is particularly suitable for a very simple sauce, as given here.

Step one If using salted anchovies, soak them in water for 30 minutes. Dry the anchovies on kitchen paper and remove any large bones.

Step two Heat the butter, add the garlic and the chilli, and fry very gently until the garlic starts to brown. Take the pan off the heat and add the anchovy fillets. Stir until smooth.

Step three Cook the pasta for 7–8 minutes or until al dente. Drain, adding 1–2 tablespoons of the pasta water to the anchovies, if necessary, to make a sauce. Toss the pasta with the sauce, and add the parsley.

Serves 4

10 anchovy fillets (salted or in oil)

75g (3oz) butter

1 garlic clove, peeled and very finely chopped

1 small chilli pepper, very finely chopped

350g (12oz) dried *lingue di passero* or linguine

1 tbsp very finely chopped flat-leaf parsley

Open Raviolo with Fish

This recipe is always very popular and will certainly attract the attention of dinner guests. If you wish to make it more colourful, try using two different colours of pasta.

Serves 6

1.5kg (3lb) mussels (about 48)

675g (1½ lb) fresh pasta dough (see page 7)

100g (4oz) butter

1 garlic clove, very finely chopped

175g (6oz) fresh scallops, cut into 5mm/¼ in pieces

175g (6oz) fresh salmon, cut into 5mm/¼ in pieces

175g (6oz) monkfish or any other firm white fish, cut into 5mm (¼ in) pieces

1 tbsp finely chopped parsley

1½ tbsp finely chopped dill, plus sprigs to garnish

2 tbsp dry white wine

1 egg yolk lightly beaten with ¼ tsp fresh lemon juice (optional)

1 tbsp olive oil

salt and freshly ground black pepper

Step one Scrub the mussels under cold running water, discarding any that are cracked or open. With a small sharp knife, scrape away the beards. Wash them in several changes of cold water until the water is left clean. Place in a large bowl, cover with cold water and leave to stand for 30 minutes. Drain and discard any with open shells. Place the mussels in a large pan with just enough water to cover the bottom. Cover and cook over a fairly high heat, shaking the pan from time to time, for 5 minutes or until all the shells have opened. Discard any that do not open. Drain the mussels and take the meat out of the shells.

Step two Divide the pasta dough into three equal-sized balls. Roll each out on a lightly floured surface to make three sheets of pasta, each about 25cm (10in) square by 3mm (less than ¼ in) thick. Cut each sheet into four squares, then lay the 12 squares on clean tea towels.

Step three Heat half the butter and fry the garlic for a few seconds. Add salt, pepper, the scallops, all the chopped fish and mussel meat, and fry for a few minutes until just cooked. Stir in the parsley, the chopped dill and the wine, and let the alcohol evaporate for 1 minute. If the filling mixture seems a little thin, thicken by beating in the egg yolk and lemon juice mixture.

Step four Bring a large pan of salted water to the boil, adding the oil. Place the pasta sheets in the water, one at a time, to prevent them sticking and cook for 4 minutes. Melt the remaining butter. Carefully remove the pasta and pat dry on clean tea towels. While still warm, place one pasta square on each of six warmed serving dishes. Divide the fish filling between the six dishes and place in the centre of each square. Use the remaining pasta squares to cover the filling and drizzle over the melted butter. Garnish with the dill sprigs.

Ravioloni with Fish

Monkfish, a round sea fish with a large ugly head, is native to the Mediterranean and both sides of the Atlantic. Only the tail is eaten and it is sold as fillets. Its firm white flesh has a flavour not unlike lobster and it is at its best from October to January.

Step one To make the filling, poach the monkfish and salmon together in simmering water for 12–15 minutes until cooked. Drain and roughly chop, removing any bones. Stir in the prawns, dill, egg yolks, salt and pepper and mix well.

Step two Roll out the pasta dough on a lightly floured surface to make two sheets of pasta about 50 x 25cm (20 x 10in) and about 3mm (less than ¼in) thick. Arrange 8 heaped teaspoonfuls of the filling on each pasta sheet, 6cm (2½in) apart. Cover with the other sheet of pasta. Press gently with your fingers all around the filling to seal the ravioloni shapes, without air bubbles. Cut the pasta into 7.5cm (3in) squares with a pastry wheel and lay the ravioloni on a clean tea towel. Cook the ravioloni in boiling salted water for 5–6 minutes, then drain.

Step three Melt the butter, adding the saffron powder or pounded strands. Serve two ravioloni on each plate with a little butter drizzled on top and garnish with the dill sprigs.

Serves 6

150g (5oz) monkfish

150g (5oz) fresh salmon

75g (3oz) fresh cooked and peeled prawns, roughly chopped

2 tbsp chopped dill, plus 4 sprigs, to garnish

2 egg yolks

675g (1½lb) fresh pasta dough (see page 7)

50g (2oz) butter

1 sachet saffron powder or pinch of saffron strands, pounded to a powder with a pestle and mortar

salt and freshly ground black pepper

For a video masterclass on filling pasta, go to
www.mykitchentable.co.uk/videos/fillingpasta

Orecchioni with Piquant Sauce

This pasta dish is a delicious blend of flavours – from the light saltiness of the anchovy fillets to the creamy pecorino cheese, it's a real delight.

Serves 4

100g (4oz) sun-dried tomatoes

4 anchovy fillets (salted or in oil)

3 tbsp coarsely chopped basil

3 tbsp coarsely chopped flat-leaf parsley

10g (¼ oz) capers, drained

2 garlic cloves, finely chopped

1 small chilli pepper

25g (1oz) pitted black olives

6 tbsp virgin olive oil

350g (12oz) dried *orecchioni* or use conchiglie or any large pasta

50g (2oz) freshly grated pecorino cheese

Step one Soak the sun-dried tomatoes in lukewarm water for about 1½ hours until soft and the saltiness has been removed. If using salted anchovies, soak in water for 30 minutes, then dry on kitchen paper and remove any large bones.

Step two Drain the sun-dried tomatoes and purée them in a food-processor with 2 tablespoons each of the basil and parsley, the anchovies, capers, garlic, chilli, olives, olive oil and 300ml (10fl oz) water, until the mixture is smooth and glossy.

Step three Cook the pasta in boiling salted water for around 12–14 minutes or until al dente. Meanwhile, gently simmer the tomato mixture in a pan for 5 minutes, adding a little more water if it is becoming too thick. Drain the pasta and toss with the sauce. Add the pecorino cheese, mix together well and serve with the remaining basil and parsley sprinkled on top.

Filled Pasta with Walnut Sauce

Preboggion is a mixture of the wild greens and herbs that grow freely on the Ligurian hills and is used for filling the tummy-shaped pasta which is typical of the region. You can use a combination of wild dandelion, wild beet, wild marjoram, wild borage or any other edible greens you can easily find.

Step one To make the filling, cook the greens until soft and squeeze out as much water as you can. Put in a pan with the butter, nutmeg and Parmesan and mix together until the butter has melted. Let the mixture cool, add the egg and salt, to taste, and set aside.

Step two On a floured surface, roll the pasta dough out to a thickness of 3mm (less than ¼in). Cut out 4cm (1½in) squares, putting a teaspoon of the filling in each square. Close to obtain a triangle. Take the top and fold over, then wrap the two other corners around your finger. This makes a similar shape to the familiar tortelloni.

Step three To make the sauce, put the milk, garlic, marjoram, breadcrumbs, walnuts and pine kernels in a blender. Process until you obtain a smooth mixture. Add the oil a little at a time (as when making mayonnaise) and blend. Add salt to taste and heat very gently, then put on one side.

Step four Boil the pasta in slightly salted water for 3–4 minutes. Drain and dress with the warmed walnut sauce. Decorate with a sprig of marjoram and serve immediately.

Serves 4–6

for the filling

1kg (2¼ lb) mixed wild greens (see recipe introduction)

40g (1½ oz) butter

pinch of grated nutmeg

40g (1½ oz) freshly grated Parmesan

1 egg, beaten

salt

for the pasta

300g (11 oz) fresh pasta dough (see page 7)

for the walnut sauce

250ml (8fl oz) milk

1 garlic clove

1 sprig marjoram, plus extra to garnish

2 tbsp fresh breadcrumbs

100g (4oz) walnuts

few pine kernels

500ml (18fl oz) olive oil

salt

Orecchiette with Broccoli

This home-made pasta is so good that it is well worth making extra and freezing some. Although fresh, these shapes take a little longer to cook than you might expect. You can buy ready-made, dried orecchiette from good delicatessens and some supermarkets.

Serves 4

450g (1lb) fresh or frozen broccoli

6 tbsp olive oil

75g (3oz) speck or lean smoked bacon, rinded and cut into small strips

2 garlic cloves, peeled and finely chopped

salt

300ml (10fl oz) milk

450g (1lb) fresh or dried orecchiette or conchiglie

50g (2oz) freshly grated Parmesan

freshly ground black pepper

Step one Boil the broccoli in salted water until tender and drain. Chop the broccoli very finely.

Step two Heat the oil and fry the speck or bacon until it is brown and crispy. Add the garlic and cook for another minute. Add the broccoli and salt, and then stir in the milk. Cook the sauce stirring until smooth.

Step three Cook the pasta for 6 minutes or until al dente (or for 15–18 minutes, if using dried). Drain and add to the sauce. Toss well with the Parmesan, add some black pepper and serve.

Neapolitan-style Macaroni

Maccheroncini, or *maccheroni*, was invented in the region surrounding Naples. Neapolitan food is mainly known for the use of tomatoes and very little meat. Simple ingredients are, in fact, transformed into many different dishes, but a Neapolitan sauce needs little introduction, for it has become such a cookery classic.

step one Heat the oil and fry the garlic and chilli for 2–3 minutes. Add the tomatoes and tomato purée, cover and cook gently for 10–15 minutes. Add the parsley, and salt to taste.

step two Cook the pasta for 7–8 minutes or until al dente, and drain. Toss the pasta with the sauce and sprinkle with freshly ground black pepper.

Serves 4

8 tbsp olive oil

2 garlic cloves, peeled and finely chopped

1 small chilli pepper, finely chopped

2 x 450g (1lb) cartons or bottles passata or chopped tomatoes

1 tsp concentrated tomato purée

3 tbsp roughly chopped flat-leaf parsley

salt

375g (13oz) dried *maccheroncini*, bucatini or spaghetti

freshly ground black pepper

Tagliatelle Verdi with Field Mushrooms

This recipe is especially dedicated to all those mushroom gatherers who safely collect the well-known field variety, *Agaricus bisporus*, which is found growing wild in Britain, and is related to the cultivated button mushroom. Naturally, this dish tastes better with the wild, field variety, but you can substitute the cultivated one. To make the result interesting, I use green pasta.

Serves 4

6 tbsp olive oil

2 garlic cloves, peeled and finely sliced

300g (11oz) field or button mushrooms, roughly sliced

4 tbsp dry white wine

100g (4oz) speck with fat, rinded and cut into strips

450g (1lb) fresh green tagliatelle (see page 7)

75g (3oz) freshly grated Parmesan

4 tbsp finely chopped flat-leaf parsley

salt and freshly ground black pepper

Step one Heat the oil and sweat the garlic. Add the mushroom and fry them over a low heat to extract their moisture. Pour in the wine and let it evaporate for 1–2 minutes. Add the speck, and salt and pepper to taste.

Step two Cook the pasta for 3–5 minutes or until al dente. Drain the pasta, and toss in the sauce. Serve sprinkled with the Parmesan and parsley.

Fettuccine Verdi with Walnut Sauce

From the region of Liguria in the north, this sauce makes good use of the area's local ingredients. It goes well with flat pasta, pasta shapes and even served on filled pasta. Fettuccine is the wider version of tagliatelle and is very popular in Rome.

Step one Soak the breadcrumbs in water for 10 minutes, then squeeze them dry.

Step two Immerse the walnuts or hazelnuts in hot water and try to remove as much of their brown skins as you can. Dry them on kitchen paper. Put the walnuts or hazelnuts in a mortar together with the breadcrumbs, the garlic, the pecorino cheese, salt and marjoram. Pound the ingredients with a pestle to a fine texture. Transfer the mixture to a small bowl. Slowly add the oil, stirring constantly with a spoon. Finally, stir in the yoghurt to make a smooth sauce.

Step three Cook the pasta for 5–7 minutes or until al dente. Drain the pasta and toss with the sauce. Serve with plenty of freshly ground black pepper.

Serves 4

1 tbsp fresh white breadcrumbs

150g (5oz) shelled walnuts or hazelnuts

1 small garlic clove, peeled

50g (2oz) freshly grated pecorino cheese

salt

1 tbsp chopped marjoram

6 tbsp virgin olive oil

4 tbsp strained Greek-style yoghurt

450g (1lb) fresh green fettuccine or tagliatelle (see page 7)

freshly ground black pepper

Maltagliati with Aubergine Sauce

Maltagliati means 'badly cut' and describes the irregular pieces of pasta which are cut out of the dough with a knife. This recipe is a dream, especially for vegetarians.

Serves 4

200g (7oz) aubergine

200g (7oz) carrots

6 tbsp olive oil

1 onion, peeled and finely sliced

1 garlic clove, peeled and finely chopped

1 tbsp chopped basil

2 tsp chopped fresh rosemary or 1 tsp dried rosemary

100ml (3½ fl oz) red wine

100ml (3½ fl oz) water

½ vegetable stock cube

1 tbsp finely chopped parsley

450g (1lb) fresh *maltagliati* (see page 7), or 400g (14oz) dried spaghetti or pappardelle, cut into irregular pieces

75g (3oz) freshly grated pecorino cheese

salt and freshly ground black pepper

Step one Peel the aubergine, discard the skin and cut the flesh lengthways into slices and then large matchsticks 5mm (¼in) thick. Peel the carrots and cut into similar matchsticks.

Step two Put the oil in a pan over a high heat. Add the onion, aubergine and carrots, and fry until soft, stirring continuously. Add the garlic, basil and rosemary, and cook for 5 minutes on a lower heat. Add the wine, water and the stock cube. Cook for 1–2 minutes to reduce the liquids. Add salt and pepper to taste and the parsley.

Step three Cook the pasta until it is al dente, allowing 4–5 minutes for the *maltagliati* or 5–6 minutes for the pappardelle. Toss the pasta in the sauce and serve sprinkled with the pecorino cheese.

Brandelli with Asparagus Sauce

Brandelli is the perfect pasta to make from scratch if you've never tried it before – simply tear off uneven strips and squares to make a delicious and authentic meal.

Step one Cook the asparagus in boiling water for 15–20 minutes or until tender. Remove from the pan and cut about 5cm (2in) off the top and keep warm. Cut the lower part of the stems into 1cm (½in) pieces.

Step two Heat the butter in a pan and gently fry the onion until just soft. Add the small asparagus pieces and the milk and cook for 5–6 minutes. Mash the asparagus with a fork until the sauce is smooth.

Step three To make the *brandelli*, just tear off 5cm (2in) pieces of rolled-out dough at random to form uneven pieces. Cook in boiling salted water for 3–4 minutes or until al dente, then drain. Mix with the sauce, add the Parmesan and toss well. Season to taste and serve the reserved asparagus tips as a garnish.

Serves 4

450g (1lb) large asparagus spears, peeled and trimmed

75g (3oz) butter

1 large onion, finely sliced

3 tbsp milk

450g (1lb) fresh pasta dough (see page 7)

75g (3oz) freshly grated Parmesan

salt and freshly ground black pepper

Agnolotti with Ricotta and Truffle

I've included this rather unusual recipe because, if at all possible, I would like you to have the extraordinary experience of tasting the famous white Alba truffle, or even the rather more mild, black one! As a last resort, use 1 tablespoon of truffle oil instead (from a good Italian delicatessen) and reduce the quantity of butter to 25g (1oz).

Serves 4

300g (11oz) ricotta cheese

1 tbsp each of finely chopped parsley, basil and mint, plus extra mint sprigs, to garnish

2 egg yolks

pinch of grated nutmeg

50g (2oz) freshly grated Parmesan

450g (1lb) fresh pasta dough (see page 7)

50g (2oz) butter

1 small fresh white or black truffle, very finely sliced

salt and freshly ground black pepper

Step one To make the filling, mix together the ricotta, parsley, basil, mint, egg yolks, nutmeg and half the Parmesan. Season with some salt and pepper.

Step two To make the *agnolotti*, roll out the pasta dough on a lightly floured surface to about 3mm (less than ¼in) thick. Cut the pasta into two sheets of the same size. Put teaspoons of filling on one sheet, 5cm (2in) apart. Cover with the other sheet of pasta, press gently with your fingers all round the filling to seal the shapes, without air bubbles. Cut the pasta into squares with a pastry wheel and lay them on a clean tea towel.

Step three Cook the pasta in boiling salted water for 4–5 minutes, then drain. Melt the butter and mix with the pasta. Serve sprinkled with the remaining Parmesan and the truffle slices on top. Garnish with a few sprigs of mint.

Sardinian Ravioli

It is interesting that two regions as far apart as Sardinia and the Veneto have a very similar way of shaping their home-made ravioli, and they both taste wonderful. The great footballer Gianfranco Zola was delighted when I made this dish from his home town of Orlena in Sardinia as a surprise for him. Unfortunately, the setting was less traditional – the grounds of Chelsea Football Club.

Step one To make the filling, mix the potatoes with the cheeses, oil and mint, then set aside.

Step two To make the dough, pile the flour up into a volcano shape on a work surface (marble is best) and make a large well in the centre. Put the egg yolk and about 120ml (4fl oz) of water in the well, keeping back a little water in case you don't need it all. Lightly beat the egg yolk and water together with a fork and then gradually mix in the flour with your hands, adding water if necessary, to make a soft dough. Knead well with the palms of your hands for 20 minutes, until smooth and elastic. Roll out the pasta either by hand or with a pasta machine until it is very thin – about 2mm (less than ¼ in). Cut out 10cm (4in) rounds. Knead the trimmings together, re-roll and cut out more rounds.

Step three To shape the *culurzones*, take a pasta round in one hand and place a teaspoonful of the filling mixture off centre on it. Turn up the bottom of the dough over the filling, then pinch a fold of dough over from the right and then the left side to give a pleated effect. Pinch the top together to seal. You should end up with a money-bag shape. Because the pasta is so thin, it is important to work quickly and to keep the remaining pasta rounds covered to prevent drying.

Step four Dissolve the saffron in a little hot water, then put the butter, sage leaves and saffron water in a large pan and heat until the butter has melted. Meanwhile, cook the *culurzones* in boiling water until al dente. Drain and combine with the hot butter mixture, stirring well, then serve sprinkled with the grated cheese, if you like.

Serves 6–8

pinch of saffron strands

50g (2oz) butter

8 sage leaves

freshly grated pecorino cheese or Parmesan, to serve (optional)

for the filling

800g (1¾lb) potatoes, boiled and mashed

200g (7oz) fresh *(dolce)* pecorino cheese, grated

50g (2oz) aged pecorino cheese, grated

120g (4½oz) freshly grated Parmesan

2½ tbsp extra-virgin olive oil

2½ tbsp finely chopped mint

for the dough

300g (11oz) *doppio zero* (00) flour

1 egg yolk

Baked Chickpea Gnocchi

Although this is similar in principle to gnocchi *alla romana*, I find that using chickpea flour instead of semolina makes for a much tastier dish. In Palermo, where gnocchi are fried and eaten sandwiched in bread, they would undoubtedly approve.

Serves 4

1.5 litres (2½ pints) water

salt

2 tbsp coarsely chopped parsley

250g (9oz) chickpea flour

oil, for greasing

50g (2oz) butter

1 tsp freshly grated nutmeg

40g (1½ oz) freshly grated Parmesan

freshly ground black pepper

Step one Put the water in a pan with the parsley and 15g (½oz) of salt and bring to the boil. Gradually pour in the chickpea flour, beating vigorously with a wire whisk to prevent lumps forming. Cook for 5 minutes, stirring, then pour the mixture on to an oiled surface and spread out in a layer 1cm (½in) thick. Leave until it has cooled and set.

Step two Preheat the oven to 200°C/400°F/gas 6.Cut the chickpea mixture into circles 4cm (1½in) in diameter and arrange them on an oiled baking sheet, overlapping them slightly. Dot with the butter and sprinkle the nutmeg, Parmesan and black pepper over the surface. Bake for 10 minutes, then place under a hot grill to brown the top. I use up the bits of dough left after cutting out the circles by baking them with a fresh tomato and basil sauce. I hate throwing food away!

Pumpkin Risotto

This recipe comes from the Hotel Cipriani in Venice, a very welcoming place though rather pricey! Its food, unlike that at many other 'international' hotels, reflects local eating habits, something I very much approve of. The pumpkin is undergoing a revival at the moment and Renato Piccolotto, the hotel's chef, cooks this wonderful risotto, which is as appealing to the eye as it is to the palate. It is very simple to make but, like all simple and delicate things, requires a little attention. Pumpkins are now widely available and can even be bought in pre-prepared chunks.

Step one In a pan, heat the oil and a third of the butter. Add the sprigs of rosemary, garlic and the pumpkin. The pumpkin will automatically exude some liquid and so no water needs to be added. Cook for about 20 minutes or until the pumpkin softens and dissolves. Remove the rosemary sprigs and garlic clove.

Step two In another large pan, heat half the remaining butter and fry the onion gently until soft, add the rice and stir-fry for a few minutes. Add a little of the chicken stock and then the pumpkin mixture. Add more stock until it is all used and absorbed by the rice, stirring from time to time to avoid sticking to the pan. Take off the heat and beat in the remaining butter and the Parmesan and sprinkle with the chopped rosemary and a little seasoning. If you have a spare pumpkin, de-seed, warm the inside with hot water, then drain, fill with the risotto and serve.

Serves 4

2 tbsp olive oil

90g (3½ oz) butter

4 sprigs of rosemary, 2 finely chopped and 2 whole

1 garlic clove, whole

600g (1lb 5oz) pumpkin flesh, chopped into very small chunks

1 small onion, finely chopped

300g (11oz) carnaroli rice

1 litre (1¾ pints) chicken stock

50g (2oz) freshly grated Parmesan

salt and freshly ground black pepper

Penne Timbales with Aubergines and Smoked Mozzarella Cheese

In Italy the combination of pasta and vegetables has always been made interesting. No one misses the meat in many dishes and this is a good example. It is a recipe worth cooking for several people.

Serves 6–8

450g (1lb) dried *penne lisce*

40g (1½ oz) butter, cut into pieces

200g (7oz) French beans, fresh or frozen

2 tbsp olive oil

450g (1lb) carrots, cut into large matchsticks

2 large aubergines, cut lengthways into 1cm (½ in) strips

1 garlic clove, finely chopped

pinch of grated nutmeg

2 x 300g (11oz) smoked mozzarella cheeses, cut into strips

400g (14oz) ricotta cheese

150g (5oz) freshly grated Parmesan

8 eggs, lightly beaten

salt and freshly ground black pepper

Step one Preheat the oven to 200°C/400°F/gas 6. Cook the pasta in boiling salted water for 5–6 minutes or until al dente, then drain well. Mix with the butter and set aside.

Step two Cook the beans in boiling water until tender, drain and set aside. Heat the oil and fry the carrot matchsticks until lightly browned on all sides. Add the aubergines to the pan with the garlic and fry until golden. Add a pinch of nutmeg and a little salt and pepper.

Step three Lightly butter a 20 x 25cm (8 x 10in) and 7.5cm (3in) deep ovenproof baking dish. Cover the base of the dish with a third of the cooked pasta. Top with one-third each of the beans, the carrots and aubergines, then the mozzarella and ricotta cheeses, and sprinkle with Parmesan. Repeat layering twice more, finishing with the Parmesan. Pour on the beaten eggs, which will bind the pasta together, and bake for 30 minutes until bubbling and golden. Serve at once.

The tastiest mozzarella is that which has been traditionally made from buffalo's milk. It is a soft cheese made by working the curd by hand while it is very hot to obtain a spongy, milky-textured ball. You'll find it sold in a plastic bag or wrapped in waxed paper in its own whey.

Tortiglioni with Mushrooms and Cheese

Tortiglioni is one of the larger pastas that looks like a twisted, hollow macaroni. Sometimes it goes by other names such as *ricciolo*, fusilli or *eliceh*. It is usually good with tomato-based sauces, but I would like you to try this exception. This sauce looks untidy, but tastes delicious.

Step one Soak the ceps in warm water for 20 minutes. Drain, reserving the soaking water. Squeeze the ceps dry and then finely chop.

Step two Heat the oil and gently fry the button mushrooms. Add the ceps with 2–3 tablespoons of the reserved soaking water and cook for 5 minutes. Remove from the heat and gently stir in the ricotta, fontina and pecorino cheeses and the beaten eggs. (The eggs should not be cooked but remain liquid at this stage.) Taste and add salt, if necessary, and pepper.

Step three Cook the pasta in boiling salted water for 6–7 minutes or until al dente, then drain. Return the pasta to the pan and mix well with the sauce, so that the egg just starts to thicken with the heat of the pasta. Serve immediately.

Caution *This recipe contains lightly cooked eggs.*

Serves 4

20g (¾oz) dried ceps

6 tbsp olive oil

200g (7oz) button mushrooms, finely sliced

200g (7oz) ricotta cheese, crumbled

100g (4oz) coarsely grated fontina cheese

50g (2oz) freshly grated pecorino cheese

3 eggs, lightly beaten

375g (13oz) dried *tortiglioni* or fusilli

salt and freshly ground black pepper

Farfalle with Fontina and Ceps

Fontina is a semi-soft cheese exclusive to the Val d'Aosta region in the Alps, where the herds of cows graze on sweet, alpine grass all summer long. No wonder the result is a deliciously sweet, melting cheese, which is pale cream with a red rind. It is classed as a table cheese, but is also used for cooking. Be sure it is the real version and not an imitation.

Serves 4

200g (7oz) fresh ceps or shiitake mushrooms, sliced, or 20g (¾oz) dried ceps

75g (3oz) butter

1 small onion, finely chopped

400g (14oz) creamed or pulped tomatoes

6–8 basil leaves, chopped

375g (13oz) dried farfalle

200g (7oz) coarsely grated fontina cheese

75g (3oz) freshly grated Parmesan, to serve

salt and freshly ground black pepper

Step one If using dried ceps, soak in warm water for around 20 minutes, then drain. Squeeze dry, then finely chop.

Step two Heat the butter and fry the onion until golden. Add the ceps or shiitake mushrooms and fry for 2 minutes. Stir in the tomatoes, add the basil leaves and cook for 5 minutes.

Step three Cook the pasta in boiling salted water for around 8–9 minutes or until al dente. Add the fontina cheese to the sauce, with salt and pepper to taste. If necessary, gently heat the cheese through, so that it melts before you toss the drained pasta with the sauce. Serve sprinkled with a little Parmesan.

Wild Mushroom Salad

Every time I return from a *funghi* hunt with just a few bits and pieces, I enjoy this salad. It is delicious made with chanterelles or morels to which you can add a few cultivated shiitake, oyster or button mushrooms. Before picking wild mushrooms, always consult a reliable reference book.

Step one Bring a pot of slightly salted water to the boil. Prepare the mushrooms by cleaning them and then discarding any tough and non-presentable pieces. Throw into the boiling water and cook for 5 minutes, then drain.

Step two Heat the oil in a pan and gently fry the garlic and chilli for a minute. Add the mushrooms, stir-fry for a minute or so, add salt and the chopped parsley. Allow to cool. Serve with lemon halves and a sprinkling of parsley.

Serves 4

675g (1½ lb) mixed funghi

6 tbsp olive oil

2 garlic cloves, finely chopped

1 red chilli pepper, finely chopped

2 tbsp coarsely chopped flat-leaf parsley

2 lemons, cut into halves

salt

Stuffed Baby Artichokes

The origin of this recipe must come from the Jewish ghetto in Rome where kosher food was the rule. These are popular with a lot of my Jewish friends. During cooking, the artichokes should be practically covered with olive oil, but that is an expensive way of using the oil. Alternatively, you can put 1cm (½in) in the bottom of the pan, then add sufficient water to push the level of the oil higher. This allows the temperature to be controlled more easily. Three artichokes per person is a wonderful starter and they are very good as part of an antipasto.

Serves 4

12 baby artichokes

juice of 1 lemon

for the stuffing

120g (4½ oz) stale white breadcrumbs

150ml (5fl oz) milk

1 tbsp finely chopped flat-leaf parsley

¼ garlic clove, crushed

1 tbsp freshly grated Parmesan

½ tbsp drained capers

extra-virgin olive oil

salt and freshly ground black pepper

Step one Trim the artichokes, cutting off the top third and trimming around the base to remove all the tough leaves. Cut out any choke, making a hollow in the centre which will hold the stuffing. Plunge into a bowl of water acidulated with lemon juice to prevent discolouration.

Step two To make the stuffing, soak the breadcrumbs with the milk and squeeze out the moisture with your hands. Mix with the remaining stuffing ingredients and season with a large pinch of salt and pepper.

Step three Fill the artichokes with the stuffing and pack side-by-side in a pan. The size of the pan is important as the artichokes must fit closely together. Drizzle the artichokes with a thin stream of oil and fill the base of the pan with 1cm (½in) depth. Add water to within 1cm (½in) of the top of the artichokes. Cover with a lid and simmer for about 20–30 minutes until tender. They are cooked when a knife pierces the artichokes easily. Cool a little and serve.

Summer Bread Salad

Here is a simple recipe that includes all the elements of the healthy Mediterranean diet. The ingredients are almost always available in a Southern Italian household and do not cost very much. My mother used leftover bread, dried in the oven the better to absorb the juice of the ripe tomatoes. Ideal as a starter on a summer's day.

Step one Soften the dried bread in a little cold water, then reduce it to coarse crumbs. Put the breadcrumbs, tomatoes, spring onions, yellow pepper, garlic, olives and basil leaves in a bowl and mix well.

Step two Add the oil and vinegar and season with a little salt and pepper. Serve garnished with the anchovies and a sprig of basil.

Serves 4

8 slices of white, country-style bread, dried in a low oven

300g (11oz) cherry tomatoes, cut into quarters

1 bunch of spring onions, finely chopped

1 yellow pepper, cut into small cubes

1 garlic clove, very finely chopped

20 green olives, pitted and halved

20 basil leaves, plus sprigs to garnish

120ml (4fl oz) virgin olive oil

1 tablespoon strong red wine vinegar

8 anchovy fillets, quartered

salt and freshly ground black pepper

Rolled Sun-dried Tomatoes

Choose very large sun-dried tomatoes for this dish in order to roll them up with the filling. Sun-dried tomatoes can be used in various ways or enjoyed plain as a snack. However, they are quite salty so it is best to soak them before use in two parts vinegar to one part water for an hour or so, then drain and pat dry. They can then be flavoured with basil, oregano, garlic or chilli and covered with olive oil to be eaten later on. Alternatively try this recipe.

Makes 20

20 large sun-dried tomatoes (leave the halves of each tomato attached)

1 tsp dried oregano

4 tbsp extra-virgin olive oil

1 tbsp salted capers, soaked in water for 10 minutes, then drained

1 tbsp mint leaves

20 anchovy fillets in oil

Step one Desalt and soften the sun-dried tomatoes as described above. Sprinkle them with the oregano and oil. Open out the tomato halves and place a few capers, mint leaves and an anchovy fillet in each tomato. Roll up to enclose the filling. Spear each roll with a cocktail stick to serve, if liked.

For more recipes from My Kitchen Table, sign up for our newsletter at www.mykitchentable.co.uk/newsletter

Aubergine Rolls

Aubergines are greatly enjoyed in Puglia, Calabria, Sicily and Basilicata, and naturally many recipes for them have developed. This is one of the simplest and tastiest.

Step one Preheat the oven to 200°C/400°F/gas 6. Cook the aubergine slices in boiling salted water for 2 minutes, then drain and pat dry (this prevents them absorbing too much oil when fried). Heat some oil in a large frying pan and fry the aubergine slices until brown on both sides. Lay the slices on a work surface.

Step two Mix together the toasted breadcrumbs, olives, half the pecorino cheese and the tomato, then season to taste with salt and pepper. Spread the mixture over the aubergine slices, place a basil leaf on top of each one and roll up, securing the rolls with a wooden cocktail stick.

Step three Place the rolls on a baking sheet, sprinkle the rest of the pecorino cheese over them and bake for 10 minutes. They can be eaten hot or cold.

Serves 4

12 long slices of aubergine, 5mm (¼ in) thick

olive oil for frying

10 tbsp fresh breadcrumbs, lightly toasted

12 olives, pitted and coarsely chopped

6 tbsp coarsely grated pecorino cheese

1 tomato, very finely chopped

12 basil leaves

salt and freshly ground black pepper

Stuffed Mushrooms

Mushrooms are a much-loved seasonal speciality all over Italy, including the south. Recently the cultivated mushroom has been gaining popularity, especially when composing a decent selection of antipasti.

Makes 12

12 open-cap mushrooms, about 4cm (1½ in) in diameter

5 tbsp fresh breadcrumbs

½ garlic clove, very finely chopped

4 tbsp freshly grated Parmesan

2 eggs

1 tbsp chopped marjoram

2 tbsp dried breadcrumbs

4 tbsp olive oil

salt and freshly ground black pepper

Step one Preheat the oven to 220°C/425°F/gas 7. Remove and discard the mushroom stalks. Mix together the fresh breadcrumbs, garlic, Parmesan, eggs, marjoram and salt and pepper and use to stuff the mushroom caps.

Step two Place the mushrooms stuffed-side up on an oiled baking sheet. Sprinkle with the dried breadcrumbs and drizzle with the oil. Bake for 15 minutes, until the mushrooms are heated through and the filling is lightly browned.

Fried and Marinated Courgettes and Aubergines

In the south, and particularly in Campania and Puglia, antipasti are almost always served with some pickled vegetables such as *giardiniera* or some fried and marinated vegetables such as these courgettes and aubergines. They make a delicious snack or accompaniment to cold roast meat.

Step one Blanch the aubergine slices in boiling salted water for 1 minute, then drain and pat dry (this prevents them absorbing too much oil when they are fried).

Step two Heat some oil in a large frying pan and lightly fry the aubergines and courgettes in batches until brown on each side. Put them in a dish, sprinkle with salt, then add the mint, oil, vinegar and garlic. Mix well and leave to marinate for at least 2 hours.

Serves 4

2 aubergines, cut into slices 5mm (¼ in) thick

olive oil for shallow-frying

4 courgettes, cut into slices 5mm (¼ in) thick

1 bunch mint, roughly chopped

4 tbsp olive oil

1 tbsp white wine vinegar

1 garlic clove, coarsely chopped

salt

For a video masterclass on knife skills, go to
www.mykitchentable.co.uk/videos/knifeskills

191

Almond Peppers

This is one of many ways of preparing peppers in Sicily, where they are also served raw, roasted, sautéed and even air-dried.

Serves 4

4 tbsp olive oil

2 yellow peppers, cut into strips

2 red peppers, cut into strips

2 tbsp white wine vinegar

1 tsp sugar

40g (1½ oz) raisins

40g (1½ oz) split almonds

150g (5oz) passata or chopped tomatoes

salt and freshly ground black pepper

Step one Heat the oil in a large pan and add the peppers. Fry on a gentle heat for about 10 minutes, stirring from time to time until softened. Then add all the remaining ingredients and cook for a further 10 minutes. Season to taste. Serve hot, warm or even cold on a summer day.

Mozzarella with Olive Oil

Besides being used in many cooked dishes, mozzarella is eaten both as an antipasto and after a meal as the cheese course. The best is made with buffalo's milk, and comes from the south.

Step one Arrange the mozzarella slices on a plate. Drizzle with the oil and season with salt and pepper. Serve with *taralli* or *grissini*. You could add a few slices of tomato and some basil leaves to make the well-known dish *insalata caprese*.

Serves 4

2 very fresh buffalo mozzarella, cut into slices 1cm (½ in) thick

3 tbsp extra-virgin olive oil

salt and freshly ground black pepper

Mixed Preserved Meat

In the past, the preservation of meat prolonged the use of slaughtered animals, especially pigs, which were made into salami and hams. Now that we all have fridges and freezers and the need for preservation is no longer so vital, salami, hams and preserved meats are made simply because they are delicious either as a snack or, as we eat them in Italy, especially in the north, as an antipasto. They are enriched by a few pickles, like preserved mushrooms, and eaten with grissini.

Serves 4

300g (11oz) mixed cooked hams and salamis (such as Milano, Napoli, culatello, salsiccia, calabra, capicolla, prosciutto, speck, bresaola and mortadella)

Step one Arrange the meats on individual plates, overlapping the slices and serve with some pickles of your choice and accompanied by grissini.

Mixed Shellfish

This antipasto is served in just about every coastal restaurant in Italy, where the local seafood is very fresh indeed. The shellfish are cooked just long enough to open and release their juices into the pan, giving this dish a real flavour of the sea. Combined with the oil and wine, the juice is so delicious that you will want to mop it all up from your plate with a piece of bread. Sea dates and sea truffles are considered real delicacies in Italy, but are hard to find elsewhere. Sea dates actually look like dates and are related to mussels, while sea truffles are similar to clams. Other shellfish could be used, such as scallops and mussels.

Step one Scrub the molluscs under cold running water, discarding any open ones that don't close when tapped on a work surface.

Step two Heat the oil in a large pan and add all the shellfish. Pour in the wine and cover the pan. Cook over a medium–high heat for a few minutes, shaking the pan from time to time, until all the mollusc shells are open and the prawns are dark pink. Discard any shells that don't open during cooking. Stir in the parsley and abundant black pepper, then serve with lemon wedges.

Serves 4

2kg (4½ lb) mixed shellfish, such as clams, prawns, sea dates and sea truffles

6 tbsp olive oil

6 tbsp dry white wine

2 tbsp finely chopped parsley

lemon wedges, to serve

freshly ground black pepper

Bottarga with Lemon

Although *bottarga* is typical of both Sardinia and Sicily, it seems to have had Greek origins. Salting and drying fish – or in this case its roe – is an ancient method of preserving. *Bottarga*, particularly tuna *bottarga*, commands very high prices, but nevertheless, it is enjoyed by the rich and, in small quantities, by the less fortunate. Here it is served with a simple dressing, but it can also be eaten with scrambled eggs or grated over pasta like Parmesan.

Serves 4

200g (7oz) tuna or mullet *bottarga*, thinly sliced

juice of 1 lemon

4 tbsp olive oil

freshly ground black pepper

Step one Arrange the *bottarga* slices on serving plates. Drizzle with the lemon juice and oil and sprinkle with freshly ground black pepper. Serve with bread – I like it with a buttered slice of crusty bread.

KITCHEN TABLE

Have you made this recipe? Tell us what you think at www.mykitchentable.co.uk/blog

Laguna Seafood Salad

In Venice, I found the greatest choice of seafood I have ever seen for this dish. The method is relatively easy to follow, but the availability of different types of seafood could provide some problems. You can substitute some of the ingredients mentioned with other available types of fish – the important thing is freshness.

Step one Clean the mussels, razor shells and clams and put in a pan with 2 tablespoons of the oil, and the garlic and parsley. Cover with a lid and cook until all the shells have opened and the flesh can be taken out easily. Discard the empty shells and any others which haven't opened and strain off the juice.

Step two Clean the squid, octopus and cuttlefish well, removing the ink from the inside of the cuttlefish. Wash well and boil for about 10–20 minutes or until tender. In a separate pan, put the prawns in boiling water for 6–7 minutes and the scallops for about 3–4 minutes. Peel the prawns.

Step three When all the fish is cooked, drain and mix together in a large bowl. Allow to cool. Slice the spring onions very finely and add to the bowl. Make a dressing from the juice of the cooked mussels, lemon juice, the remaining oil, salt and pepper and mix with the fish. Garnish with empty shells as artistically as you like!

Serves 6

1.5kg (3lb) mussels

550g (1¼ lb) razor shells

1.5kg (3lb) clams

8 tbsp extra-virgin olive oil

1 garlic clove, finely chopped

3 tbsp coarsely chopped flat-leaf parsley

400g (14oz) small squid

3 or 4 small octopus

550g (1¼ lb) cuttlefish

400g (14oz) raw tiger prawns

400g (14oz) scallops, shelled

1 bunch spring onions

juice of 2 lemons

salt and freshly ground black pepper

Anchovies in Green Sauce

This was the contribution of my elder sister, Grazia, to a family reunion meal in Ivrea, and it is a very typical Piemontese speciality – delicious either as part of an antipasto or as a snack for when you feel a little peckish. It requires a little work, filleting salted anchovies, to get the best taste, so it is better to prepare enough to enjoy for some time. Of course you can use tinned fillets of anchovies in oil; in this case, it takes only a minute to make as much as you want. To make it even quicker to prepare, simply place all the ingredients in a liquidiser and blend until smooth. Serve with plenty of bread.

Serves 6

300g (11oz) anchovy fillets,cleaned weight

200g (7oz) finely chopped parsley

2 whole chilli peppers, finely chopped

2 garlic cloves, finely chopped

1 tbsp capers, finely chopped

4 small gherkins, finely chopped

sufficient olive oil for covering

Step one Fillet the anchovies, if necessary. Combine the parsley, chillies, garlic, capers and gherkins with the oil. Take a china bowl and build alternate layers of anchovies and the green herb sauce until it is all used up. Chill until required. If the oil congeals in the fridge, don't worry as it will melt again once the dish is taken out.

10 9 8 7 6 5 4

Published in 2011 by BBC Books, an imprint of
Ebury Publishing
A Random House Group company

Recipes © Antonio Carluccio 2011
Book design © Woodlands Books Ltd 2011

All recipes contained in this book first appeared in
Passion for Pasta (1993), *Antonio Carluccio's Italian Feast*
(1996), *Antonio Carluccio's Southern Italian Feast* (1998)
and *Antonio Carluccio Cooks Pasta* (1999)

Antonio Carluccio has asserted his right to be identified
as the author of this Work in accordance with the
Copyright, Designs and Patents Act 1988

The Random House Group Limited
Reg. No. 954009

Addresses for companies within the Random House
Group can be found at www.randomhouse.co.uk

A CIP catalogue record for this book is available from the
British Library

The Random House Group Limited supports the
Forest Stewardship Council (FSC®), the leading
international forest certification organisation.
Our books carrying the FSC label are printed
on FSC® certified paper. FSC is the only forest
certification scheme endorsed by the leading
environmental organisations, including Greenpeace.
Our paper procurement policy can be found at
www.randomhouse.co.uk/environment

To buy books by your favourite authors and register for
offers visit www.rbooks.co.uk

Printed and bound in the UK by Butler, Tanner and
Dennis Ltd

Colour origination by AltaImage

Commissioning Editor: Muna Reyal

Project Editor: Joe Cottington

Designer: Lucy Stephens

Photographer: William Reavell © Woodlands Books
Ltd 2011 (see also credits below)

Food Stylists: Katie Giovanni, Annie Rigg, Silvana Franco
and Sarah Ramsbottom

Props Stylists: Liz Belton and Helen Payne

Copy-editor: Anne Newman

Production: Helen Everson

Photograph on page 4 by Alastair Hendy © Alastair
Hendy 2011
Photographs on pages 18, 21, 54, 62, 117, 145, 146, 162,
165, 173 by Juliet Piddington © Woodlands Books Ltd 2011
Photographs on pages 109, 169, 190, 193, 198 by Philip
Webb © Woodlands Books Ltd 2011

ISBN: 9781849901482

MIX
Paper from
responsible sources
FSC® C023561
www.fsc.org